MW01700558

The Children's Home

The Children's Home

Stories and Poems

Sharon Lia Robinson

Dancing Heart Press

Cover: The author, close-up, age eight, Vista Del Mar Jewish Children's Home beach trip to Santa Monica, California, May, 1958.

Back Cover: Sharon Lia Robinson in Port Townsend, Washington. Photograph by Steven R. Johnson.

ISBN: 978-0-9964542-1-6

This book is available through Sheriar Books
www.sheriarbooks.com
843-272-1339

Published by
Dancing Heart Press
P.O. Box 895
Port Townsend, WA 98368
www.sharonrobinson.org

Dancing Heart Press is committed to publishing poetry, stories and visual art by Sharon Lia Robinson.

Also by the author:
Wayward Star, Devotional Poems

DISCLAIMER

This book is inspired by a true story and is based on the author's memory and imagination. She conveys her recollection of actual childhood episodes along with some that are make-believe. Yet the make-believe details convey the re-creation, the completion and the depth of her experience. This book is her story of finding the missing places, a combination of fact, fantasy and fiction. The places that inspire this story are Vista Del Mar Children's Home and the David and Margaret Children's Home, where the author lived as a child for several years. The stories and memories are inspired by her years at these children's homes, 1957–1960.

Today Vista Del Mar is thriving and appears, from my research, to have wonderful resources for the children who live there. In writing these stories I began to have a strong sense that my birth father's complaints to various officials while I was there were a catalyst for the changes that followed. The years when major improvements were initiated seem to have developed soon after I was informed that I would be leaving the home. Today, at Vista Del Mar, there is a much improved and dynamic program of social services, the arts, education and emotional health resources. With more awareness, the children's home is a better place.

For Meher Baba, the Awakener

Holy Companion
Eternal Guest
Lord and Friend

Soy una historia

Una memoria que se inventa

Nunca estoy solo

Hablo siempre contigo Hablas siempre conmigo

A oscuras voy y planto signos

I am a history

A memory inventing itself

I am never alone

I speak with you always

You speak with me always

I move in the dark

I plant signs

Octavio Paz

Vrindaban, p. 102–103

Selected Poems, 1979

Lysander Kemp, translation

Penguin Books

Acknowledgements and Special Thanks

To my social worker, Martina Abba-Richard, for her encouragement and prayers.

For David Cumberland (aka David Johnson), editor Karen Stimson and Dr. Fred Whitehead, who have all imparted to me that the children's home experience is significant.

For readers and advisors Judy Alexander, Shelley Allan-Cole, Brother John Blazo, M.M., Val Johnstone, Debra Lessin, Reverend Jane Mckann, Dr. Marsha Milburn Madigan and Margaret D. McGee.

For the two children's homes where I was a child resident,
Vista Del Mar Children's Home, Los Angeles, California, 1957–1960
David and Margaret Children's Home, La Verne, California, 1960.

Thank you to CBC Radio for First Nations documentaries of Canadian residential schools and reconciliation.

Dr. Viktor E. Frankl, Logotherapy and Existential Analysis.

Janet Goldenbogen-Self (RN, Intuitive Counselor), Steven R. Johnson (visual artist), Bonnie Masi (Family Constellation Gatherings), Carol Messier, Ingrid Musson, Kenton Pierce (USN corpsman, Vietnam).

For St. Mary Star of the Sea, St. Paul's Episcopal Church and Bet Shira.
Dr. Meredith Moon, (Jungian dream work and Spiritual Direction).

Laura Smith of Sheriar Books for suggesting I use the word victor for myself when writing this book.

With love and appreciation for the holy angelic beings amongst us, seen yet unseen.

And for the music of Father Antonio Vivaldi.

Amen.

TABLE OF CONTENTS

ILLUSTRATIONS

FOREWORD

Sharon Lia Robinson is a deeply moving author who shares her experience of finding her way as a young child in adverse circumstances. Her stories of her journey towards faith, trust, and purpose inspire us to find the same within ourselves.

Sharon's spiritual teacher, Meher Baba, is well-known to me, and in fact is the reason that our paths crossed. Living an hour or so away from Sharon in the Pacific Northwest, we connected only after I moved to Tucson, via Meher Baba's grace.

Sharon's explorations via the written word and poetic expression reflect to us an opportunity to explore our own depths of experience, imagination, and meaning.

Thank you, Sharon, for sharing yourself with us in a way that intensely inspires our own seeing into the mystery of life. The replacing of memories with a sense of Love is the gift of your book.

With Gratitude,
Marsha Milburn Madigan, MD
Tucson, Arizona
February 27, 2021

AUTHOR'S INTRODUCTION

Leaving Home

The prayer God hears is the prayer of the heart, that raising of the heart, that suffering of the heart, that is what God pays attention to.

— Meher Baba, July, 1956, London

When I was seven years old I was told to pack one suitcase, with only one doll. I remember I was told I was going to a place "like summer camp" for a few days, a few weeks or so. I was driven there by a social worker. After three months of total family separation and another two years of minimal parental visits, I was able to leave Vista Del Mar Jewish Children's Home. I was thankfully transferred to a better children's home where I thrived.

There I met Ruth and Rabbi Michael A. Robinson, who invited me to visit with them and then asked me to join their family. I lived with the Robinson family in Croton-on-Hudson, New York. I later found out that Croton is the village where my spiritual teacher Meher Baba stayed years earlier, on His first journey to the United States in 1931 and again in 1932. Known previously as Harmon-on-Hudson, that is where He had His first ashram in America. The privately owned house where He stayed at that time, and also in 1932, is still located only two miles as the crow flies from where I lived and grew up in Croton.

In this collection of events from my experience and imagination, I share how I found God in childhood and His gifts to me of spiritual faith, trust and creative expression. I share the way I found, in those early years, the faith, trust and purpose, the strength and resilience that sustains me.

Following adverse family circumstances I lived in Vista Del Mar Children's Home (age seven to age ten) where I was not allowed to have regular family visits. Through Divine Intervention and the efforts of my birth father, I was transferred to a Methodist Children's Home, a farm and loving family-like atmosphere. There, more people cared about me and I thrived.

At that time, age ten, I was the only Jewish child in the Methodist place. On Sundays, we each visited the individual places of worship for our faith. And my place was at the Sunday school of the Reform Jewish temple in Pomona, California. That is the way that I met Ruth and Rabbi Michael A. Robinson and their two young children, Joel and Jude.

I can still recall the wonder and anticipation I felt as a child of ten, being able to visit for a Sunday or a weekend overnight at a real home after so many years.

One day, after I had been visiting the Robinson family for several months or so, they told me that Mike was traveling to a small village in New York state, to be interviewed for the rabbinate.

Soon, I was invited to speak with Mrs. Gage, the social worker on the staff of the David and Margaret Home. "I have a surprise for you," she said. "If you like, you may go to New York to live with the Robinsons."

I immediately said yes. Because I wanted to be with them, to live with a real family once again. Several months later, the Robinson family and I were on a plane to New York, en route to the village of Croton-on-Hudson, New York. I became their foster child and they later adopted me.

Yet the years of turmoil before my adoption by the Robinsons continued to be a place of inner questioning, exploration, social and emotional challenge. As I moved forward on so many levels, I was still emotionally wounded. And yet, I know that I found something at Vista, something that made me different. These poems and stories explore, through memory, experience and imagination, the road to wholeness, adventures and paz. I am grateful that these stories have finally found their way to the printed page.

a way to make up
make believe
a way to be me

in the secret
hideaway

of a long lost
fantasy

and the wish
for a better reality

in a way this book is a tribute to those years
the formerly lost years are now given voice

my voice
in new yet old
memory faith imagination

now I too
am alone with Vivaldi

now I too
walk with the clouds
as I see them

now I too
am alone
in His likeness

Sharon Lia Robinson
Port Townsend, Washington
February 22, 2021

1. Little Moments

Love is the reflection of God's unity in the world of duality. It constitutes the entire significance of creation.

— Meher Baba, *Discourses*

How I Began to Write *The Children's Home*

alongside
the lucky guidance
of devas music and musicians

a web of meanderings
alone and together
a thread of reflection and memory

a mystery
a secret message embellished
my own imaginary kaleidoscope

imaginative interpretation
embellished fact and exploration
imagination fragmentation my life

When, as a young college student, I met the poet David Cumberland, I found a new realm of belonging. A friend and mentor, a poetry lifeline.

Thank you to David Cumberland for letting me know of Edward Dahlberg's autobiography, *Because I Was Flesh*, with the chapters on Dahlberg's life in the Jewish orphanage, and our friend, Fred Whitehead, sending me the Dahlberg book again, decades later.

The poet David Cumberland (born David Johnson) is a special and unique friend who gave me the sense of an awareness, significance and value in my early experience in the two children's homes. In his subtle yet direct and intense way, in gentle explanations that I could appreciate, the insights from David helped me to see that perhaps I had lived through more than simply a path to my psychotherapist's office in search of letting go and moving on.

David showed me the autobiography *Because I Was Flesh* by Edward Dahlberg when I told him that I had lived in two children's homes. The book was published in 1964 by New Directions. Yet even though Edward Dahlberg lived in the Jewish Orphan Asylum in Cleveland, Ohio, between 1912–1917, his experiences in the Jewish orphanage resonate with mine.

Around 1977, David encouraged me to read the book, *Because I Was Flesh*, (Part III is about Dahlberg's life in the orphanage). This was the first time anyone had brought to my attention the written stories of someone else in a home. I began to acknowledge that this experience had meaning and purpose for me in ways I needed to explore.

David loaned me the book. Later he would ask me if Dahlberg's orphanage experience resonated with my experience. At first I briefly hesitated, then said that in a way, it certainly did. "That's what I thought would happen," David smiled, a twinkle of mystery and mischief in his eyes. "You are finding yourself," he said.

David was one of the first people who helped me to realize the meaning of this experience as being central to my life. I feel that he had a personal interest and commitment in speaking with me about my life there. And he took the time to help me to recognize the significance of my experience. This interest expanded, paralleled and intertwined in the bond I developed with him as friend and mentor, and in his love of music, literature, art and social justice. He also saw the damage that had been done to me — that the inner wound was something I carried that permeated my very soul.

I believe that he was my witness, someone who, by their presence, is there to validate and to value the times of endurance, to have compassion and to acknowledge that woundedness. This he saw as my friend and in his own life and poetry.

Through his friendship and our discussions, David Cumberland helped me to become aware in a new way of my early life in the children's homes and to be able to more fully understand for myself the importance for this time in my life. The book by Edward Dahlberg provided me with the rare sense of connection I had to another writer who had lived in a children's home. Dahlberg was in a Jewish orphanage and I was in a Jewish children's home and then a Methodist one. The recommendation by David was very valuable since the book is an emotional and literary insight to mirror my own reflections.

> the sameness and echoes of my own experiences
> even though the decades were different

Years later, when our friend Fred Whitehead again mentioned Dahlberg I told him of the profound influence of David's talks with me. Fred then sent me Dahlberg's book *Because I Was Flesh.*

Fred's encouragement was a catalyst to help me develop some of the themes in this book and I began to share some of these stories with him. One of the first stories I showed him was *Sundays at the Children's Home*, in June 2017. As I wrote more stories, I came to understand the importance of the children's home experience in my life.

Fred also mentioned that the composer Father Antonio Vivaldi was, for many years, the music director and composer in a girl's orphanage and that Vivaldi was known as "the red priest" because of his hair. Fred sent me Vivaldi's two *Glorias*, originally written to be sung and played by the children who were residents at the orphanage.

"Vivaldi was on the staff of a mostly girl's orphan school in Venice, and clearly he was deeply inspired by their joyful voices, innocent, lovely..." Fred also mentioned how David liked Father Antonio Vivaldi's nickname, "il Prete Rosso, 'the red priest,' but it was his red hair, not his politics (off by a few centuries on that) that earned it."

David often listened to classical music
as a way to center himself
as a way to find peace
and many of the symphonies
I listened to with him
no doubt were also healing me too

Listening to the music of Vivaldi, knowing of Vivaldi's place in the girl's orphanage and of David's connection to Vivaldi helped me to find my early voice for this collection. The Gloria recordings that Fred sent and the story he told me of Father Vivaldi's musical teachings in the orphanage are helpful as I am able to imagine the gift of music that God gave Vivaldi to nurture the children there. And thus me too.

A Gift of Faith

The Mysterious Catholic connection comes to life again during the writing of these stories. I have often been interested in the Catholic Mass and visiting Catholic churches. Many of the poems in my book *Wayward Star, Devotional Poems* were developed during my times of prayer at the Catholic Church down the road from me, St. Mary Star of the Sea. I had found a place to pray and to develop friendships within walking distance to where I live. This close proximity to the church is a blessing.

Yet my deep and long time interest in Catholicism continued to be a source of mystery to me. This connection seemed more intense than simply knowing I had walked past a convent on my way "home" to Vista Del Mar from the nearby public school.

I didn't understand my connection in the Catholic Church until I began unearthing the mysteries of my lost years at Vista Del Mar Children's Home. In July 2018, while reconnecting with some of the now adults who had also lived at Vista as children, I discovered to my surprise that as a child at Vista Del Mar, there were several Catholic influences. I verified with some of the former child residents my vivid memories of walking "home" past the convent. I learned the name of the Catholic order was Nazareth, and contacted them as well.

While walking back to the Jewish children's home from public school, I found an out of the way path past the Nazareth Convent.

Walking through the convent grounds I may have glimpsed the nuns and spoke with them occasionally. Today, the sense of safety, beauty and mystery I experienced there gives me a feeling of gratitude and of admiration for the Catholic faith. My walk past the convent, I feel, was an early insight for me of the feeling of a peaceful refuge and of God's love. I have a strong feeling that my lifelong connection to Catholicism was nurtured in those days.

I also found out that one of our more caring and compassionate house parents, Milt Davis, was Catholic and that when we said our

Jewish dinner time prayers in Cottage Eleven and during the large Passover gatherings for the entire home, he used to make the sign of the cross. This significant discovery shed light on some of my own memories of him.

My third surprise was again connecting with my roommate and friend in Cottage Eleven, the girl next to me in our small dormitory during our several years there. Catherine James came to the home at almost exactly the same time that I did. Speaking with her in 2018, I found out that although she is Catholic, she had been permitted to live at Vista because of a family connection. At the time, this was most unusual.

When I asked her, "When we were children, did you speak to me of Jesus?" she said, "Yes, I believe I must have, because He was my Savior."

Praying to God and trusting in Him is what I believe sustained me at Vista Del Mar Children's Home, when my family visits were erratic, chaotic and unpredictable. I believe that God placed me next to this child to learn about Jesus and to have compassion for the other, for she was an outsider, being the only non-Jewish child.

I believe God placed us together so that I could have the experience of her faith, our shared sorrow, and the times that she may have spoken to me longingly of Jesus with hope.

While writing my book, *Wayward Star, Devotional Poems*, I felt guided to include in that book two short passages about my early years in the Jewish children's home, Vista Del Mar. The two stories are *My Raggedy Ann Doll*, and *A Chant for Mrs. T*. These two stories resonate with the devotional poems. Now I see and know that Vista is a place where I learned compassion for the outsider, including myself. When a child at Vista was different, that was the cross they carried.

When I included two children's home stories in my 2017 book, *Wayward Star, Devotional Poems*, I didn't see a connection between those stories and my prayer life. Yet at Vista Del Mar, the cross was my safety, a secret perhaps, a place in my heart. Obscured as a young woman by rebellion and loss, this faith was later resurrected as I began to find God once again as Meher Baba.

A Beacon of Light

I believe that during the bleak years at Vista the spark of love emanating from these Catholic influences provided a kindly and loving spiritual sustenance and sense of assurance for me. I recently learned that a houseparent who worked with the older children was also Catholic and attended Mass at the neighboring Nazareth convent. I sense that this housemother, the convent nuns and houseparent Milt Davis prayed for us kids. And that we felt their prayers. This is the faith of my childhood, the crux.

On my walks past the Nazareth Convent, I was able to explore nature and mystery and to reach out into the unknown to release my fear. During those lost years, prayers from these Catholic sources is what sustained me. My connection at this time in my life to Catholicism is not from rites, rituals, dogma or a sense that I need to convert to the Catholic faith.

My sense of hope, of love, of survival is what was nurtured for me by the prayerful Catholics that I met and whose love I felt during the years I lived at Vista Del Mar. Today the mystics and saints, the value of contemplative life, and prayer practices such as Lectio Divina, the Rosary, the Examen and the Daily Rule continue to draw me closer to that realm. In walks and visits to my nearby Catholic church, perhaps I am still listening for the inner music of childhood meanderings past the convent near Vista.

An Independent Scholar

This story reflects my desire, as a young experimental artist, to find an outer social mirror, a reflection for my life.

In the autumn of 1987, I traveled once again to northern California. Earlier that year I had finished a massage certification course at Esalen Institute, in Big Sur. Now, I was determined to find work as a massage therapist.

I was hoping to break my long-standing pattern of working part-time as a nanny, artist's model and office assistant. Even though I had also worked informally as an editor and a biographer, I felt that I was not earning enough money as a writer.

My poems, plays and stories were published and presented in alternative places like coffeehouses, small theatre spaces, or alternative and feminist journals, as a labor of love and dedication.

Therefore, when I received a financial gift from my family, I decided to go to Esalen for their first ever massage certification program.

In 1986–1987, Esalen was then in transition, as it is today.

In the evenings after dinner, I would visit the atrium — a small back room away from the main guests — where Esalen staff would socialize, play guitar, drink wine.

When the massage course finished I was staying on at Esalen, as a work scholar, and was beginning to feel accepted in the community. The usual passionate staff discussions as to whether or not Esalen is a community for artists and healers or a business to make money were taking place.

Richard Price, beloved Esalen co-founder, had passed away, in a nearby tragic hiking accident. The staff and long-time members of the community were still in deep mourning.

Many of his friends and students appeared to be feeling disillusioned with the changing scene. An arts center, moreover, was not moving forward as had been the promise of Richard Price.

By sitting in with staff in the atrium and because of my housekeeping assignments, I was learning about the inner workings of Esalen. By the time I studied there, the place was becoming more expensive and exclusive. Yet, there was also a great amount of freedom for personal exploration, meditation, self-examination.

However, my main focus was to finish my thirty massage practice sessions, rather than receive more intensive psychological help.

Yet there were times when, even while cleaning a retreatant's room, I would find one of the psychologists nearby and in the midst of vacuuming, changing the bed sheets or otherwise cleaning, I would engage in an informal therapy session.

Housekeeping was known to be one of the most physically and emotionally intense work scholar departments. We also cleaned the hot tubs that were down by the mineral springs at the baths, carried the used massage towels and massage sheets back to the laundry, did the laundry, then brought the clean towels and sheets back to the baths, in addition to cleaning the guest rooms.

At the end of my four-month stay at Esalen, I did some traveling in Mexico, and then I returned to the real world, working as a nanny and getting certified in infant massage. The adjustment was not easy. I had hoped to stay on at Esalen, perhaps getting a scholarship to study Continuum Movement, or being able to help at the Gazebo, the day care place for children. I was not chosen.

When I again traveled to northern California in the fall of 1987, hoping to find a place to live and to begin my practice as a massage therapist, a curious incident occurred. I began to feel a slight strain in my right arm. Gradually this ache became so intense that my right arm was virtually paralyzed. Although I am left-handed, I felt stranded at the hostel in Santa Cruz.

Fortunately, an emergency phone call to a family friend in Berkeley, California helped me to find a temporary place to live. Rabbi Leah Novick called her friends, who lived in North Berkeley. They had two small children and I was given free room and board in exchange for very occasional childcare.

I had a lot of time to explore Berkeley. The family lived within walking distance of the Berkeley acupuncture clinic and I was soon receiving remedial treatments for my arm strain.

The location was ideal as I could also walk to poetry readings at Black Oak Books, as well as being close to an art center, local coffee houses and the Berkeley Rose Garden.

One day, an impressive-looking man with a fancy briefcase sat at a table next to me in a coffeehouse near the Berkeley Rose Garden.

Somehow, we began to exchange pleasantries. I asked him what he had in his briefcase and if he was a university professor.

(Since my arm was actually paralyzed, I had decided I had a psychological conflict between becoming a massage therapist and continuing being my authentic self as an experimental poet, dancer and writer. I was still trying to find a way to fit into the world).

The man looked at me again — he had a sense of aloneness and independence in his manner. He said, "I am doing my own research."

I was even more curious and intrigued. I knew, even unconsciously, that none of the paths or the careers of those then prevalent around me or available suited my life experiences. I was seeking an outer link to connect to my own inner wanderings.

"What sort of research," I asked?

The man sipped his coffee, carefully and mysteriously opened his briefcase, took a pen from his lapel, and simply said to me, "I am an independent scholar." And he began leafing through his papers.

I firmly believe this brief encounter was divinely orchestrated by Meher Baba, leading me to find my own truth, my own answers to life, my own path. This phrase, "independent scholar" was a clear message of validation for my life.

Soon after that experience, my right arm, which was briefly and most mysteriously paralyzed, was healed. Through acupuncture and herbal remedies from the clinic, and just taking time to think and to relax away from the social pressure to fit in, I found some answers and resolution.

Even though my success at this point in time was not clearly understood by those around me, I had found an answer to the meaning of my life and creative work.

Following this experience in Berkeley, I reluctantly moved back to southern California where I continued to write poems and stories, coordinate poetry readings and share with people about the teachings of Meher Baba. I also worked part-time as a nanny once again.

Along the way, for many years I earnestly attempted to develop a massage practice. In southern California I met many wonderful bodyworkers and healers, and I am appreciative and grateful for our holistic exchanges and their encouragement for me as a practitioner.

Yet, I was never able to find a way to be a massage therapist or a comfortable setting for such work. The world was very different from Esalen Institute.

In 2012, I researched on a whim and there actually is an academic organization called National Coalition of Independent Scholars. Well, I am an independent scholar, since for most of my life I have been trying to unlock the inner secrets of who I am.

My own life and research is experiential, experimental, mostly based on my inner translations in creative dance, poetry, plays, stories and visual art.

Some Afterthoughts

This sunny autumn afternoon, sitting in my backyard in Port Townsend, I reflected on this story and knew that there was more that I needed to include.

When I was unable to work within certain social structures, my family were often unable to understand or to sympathize. My father, Michael, gave me an article about women poets who "make their living doing something other than poetry." My aunt said, "You have a Master's Degree, can you teach?" The casual social question, "What sort of work do you do?" haunted me for several decades.

In Encinitas, California, in 1991, I saw an article in the newspaper about post-traumatic stress disorder and veterans. At the time, I was also speaking with various Vietnam veterans in the community who had been practicing and teaching tai chi, yoga and meditation. I realized that like some of them, I had a form of PTSD from my childhood experiences. In my research I became aware of the long-term effect of brain changes on one's behavior due to trauma.

I also wrote out some of my ideas at this time for the concept of a place where people who are gifted yet face challenges may live in a community and receive social support for learning and working. I was hoping and trying to figure out how to receive funding for such a project. I was hoping that my family would help me.

I also visited several L'Arche Communities founded by Jean Vanier and did research on other communities for the developmentally disabled, such as Rudolf Steiner-based Camphill places, thinking I could possibly work and live in such a center as a support person. Yet my own challenges kept getting in the way.

I slowly realized my calling was to work on my own inner landscape, continue to create art and poems, and learn to accept myself. On February 28, 1987, while at Esalen Institute, I wrote the following poem.

Passion Flower
(passiflora coccinea)

I drink the nectar
of the passion flower

and toss the bright red petals
into the clear rocky stream

my hands touch the earth
find one smooth round stone

waterfalls dance to the ocean.

+ There is a legend that if you pick a passion flower, drink the nectar and then toss the petals while making a wish, you will actualize your dream.

11. Dolly Stories

Everyone is seeking happiness but few have it; for lasting happiness dawns only when there is complete freedom from wants.

— Meher Baba, *Discourses*

Dolly

the dolls will once again
come for tea
and play with thee
remember me

pray with me
play with them
remember me

the lovely little girl
all alone in the pool
is once again free
to walk by the sea
remember me

your faithful prince
with His midnight kiss
you will once again see
in His palace of eternity
remember me

the unknown scroll
exacts its toll
heavy karma will unroll
to clear the embers in your soul
remember me

the garden loss
exacts a cost
in measure and loss
reap and toss
remember me

the cruel fate
the insane hate
the unopened gate
remember me

the lost are found
at home unbound
at last remember me

Let this be

+

the doll with purple hair
is now a redhead
play with the dolls again
and all that was lost
again be wed
to the Divine Thread
now time for bed

remember me

The Lost Dolls

While a child resident at Vista Del Mar, I had missed my diverse collection of dolls, childhood companions and confidants that were resting on my bed the last time I had seen them. After several years at Vista Del Mar Children's Home, I was allowed to go home for one overnight weekend visit, something the other children were regularly permitted. As I glanced into the new place where my birth mother now lived, I tentatively asked her what had happened to all of my dolls.

There were cloth dolls and teddy bears, my Raggedy Ann and Raggedy Andy dolls, and several smaller chubby dolls with curly dark and light-colored hair, purchased from a hobo going door to door. There were grown-up looking dolls and baby dolls and even a porcelain doll. I used to speak with them, and sometimes they looked happy, playful, or sad and tired or hungry. There were hierarchies and categories for which ones I liked best, this changed from time to time. Sometimes they would advise me about ideas other people couldn't explain.

During the years my birth mother had visited me at Vista, I had often thought lovingly of my doll collection. Looking forward to meeting with them again after so many years was often one of the ways that my spirit of hope and imagination survived, so I could function at Vista, where the parent visits restrictions imposed on me were taking their toll.

"Oh, I gave them all away when you went to Vista," she said. "When I saw them they made me think of you, I felt sad and missed you."

"I wished you had stored them and saved them for me," I said.

"I didn't know if I would ever have the chance to give them back to you," she said. "Just having them in the house was more than I could bear."

"What about all of my books?" I asked. My mother looked sad and maybe a little evasive or embarrassed. "I gave them away for other children, since you were growing up at Vista and I thought you wouldn't need them," she said.

For decades after this experience, I felt a sense of disbelief about what my birth mother had done. Not until now do I know that what she did was for the best, no doubt it was a blessing in disguise, as I have learned to see all of my life and experiences this way. Knowing and practicing this philosophy has kept me optimistic in the face of adversity for the last several years.

A few years ago, in January 2016, my friend Ellen was giving me a ride home and I noticed she had some large boxes and bags in the back of her car. When I inquired, she mentioned she was planning to give away several bags of clothing, household items and a bag of toy pet animals for children. I asked her if we could donate a few of the pet toy animals to my social worker, who also works with children. Ellen agreed. Later, my social worker sent me a note, thanking us. The note said, "Thank you and Ellen so very much for the little toys. I think they will be finding a new home very soon. Thank you for thinking of my clients...God so bless you. Peace."

little girl dolls
that looked like me
grown-up lady dolls
with fancy clothes, jewelry and upswept hairdos
little baby dolls
with their own small blankets and pillows
resting laughing playing
whispering singing waiting for me
reunion

My Car Case

One quiet Labor Day afternoon in September 1957, a car drove up to the apartment where I lived with my birth mother, Anne. She explained to me as best she could that I was going away for awhile.

We greeted the social worker and my mother and I walked with her to her car, in the bright southern California sunlight. We placed my suitcase in the back seat alongside a smaller suitcase, called, I remember, my "car case," a 1950's small child's travel suitcase especially for me with a mirror inside.

At the last minute, the social worker asked if there was a special doll I liked, and I said "Yes, my Raggedy Ann and Raggedy Andy dolls." I was permitted to take one doll, my Raggedy Ann Doll. My mother handed me a few snacks for the car ride.

"It won't be long, I'll see you soon," said my mother.

My memory says that I saw her again after three months. My records from Vista Del Mar Children's Home, which were sent to me when I requested them in September and October of 1992, say that I saw her again after one year.

Collage Art Files

collage art files
simple treasures tucked away
in boxes dusty and obscure

today
between lunch and poetry
I sort through some of these tins

cookie tins
saved boxes from former holiday gifts to me
now reveal treasured slips of wrapping paper

beads flowers ribbons
a wedding wreath I remember
found on a lonesome park bench

one summer solstice afternoon
echoing happy decorations
that we retrieved

from a large cardboard box outside
a rented beach front cottage
found after the wedding reception

my friend and I
we couldn't understand why
such precious bits of string

handmade paper mache flowers
and multi-colored confetti
were left forgotten discarded

we were so glad to rescue
these salvaged forgotten ribbons
found meaning in the recycling

of someone else's party
saved money and got free toys
we'll use ourselves

one day soon
when the time is right
later with these tiny bits

of leftover string and colored paper
my hands make believe
make do repair restore

weaving together
real and imaginary strands
of my life

childhood dolls now speak an abstract language
their memory and loss
seeps into the special glue
on my hands
as I make a new collage.

III. The Convent Stories, A Mysterious Path

Love is the cleanser that wipes the mirror bright
and enables you to behold with increasing clarity
the indivisible entity that permeates all life.

— Meher Baba, *Life At Its Best*

A Faith Walk

"I will not leave you orphans, says the Lord; I will come back to you and your hearts will rejoice."

— John, 14:18

Several stories related to my walking past a convent on my way "home" to Vista after school or a Saturday film outing.

From living at Vista Del Mar Jewish Children's Home, one memory I have is of happiness in walking back to Cottage Eleven after public school, and walking past the Nazareth Convent. I have since felt that this early experience of seeing the nuns, in my memory and in my imagination, helps me in my faith walk and in my poems and stories of faith, based on memory, imagination and experience.

Before I found the name of the order of the convent, I began to write from my memory, alongside my imagination and my feelings. In this collection, I thus call the convent Carmelite. His Grace in permitting me to view a loving institutional environment is a loving gift of God in my memory.

"after school"

after school
I would often walk home alone
past the convent
where white sheets and blankets
flirted on the clothesline

The Nunnery Near Vista

Walking "home" alone after school or sometimes with another kid or several, we couldn't help being curious about some of the sights along the way. We would sometimes find chewing gum on the pavement and then, prompted, pool our last pennies at the candy store/delicatessen for one or two pieces of bubble gum, sharing the comics and the wrapping paper to hide the gum once we reached the children's home.

Otherwise, "Who gave you money to buy this?" "You'll rot your teeth." "You'll spoil your supper." "You'll step on it on the floor and it will be messy." All, well meaning nonsense from houseparents who maybe had no idea how enjoyable life could be with one piece of bubble gum, unwrapped and divided by three.

Also on the way home, a nunnery where the nuns were hanging out their white sheets and they smiled at me. In the wind I enjoyed seeing the sheets flying. One day a week the nuns kept silence. I was invited, in a note, to visit on a Saturday for tea. The housemother wrote back a note I carried back over there for Sister Theresa.

"She cannot visit with you because there is no one to supervise her." Silly rules that made no sense to a child or a holy sister, yet we had to suffer and obey. So the sisters simply smiled at me on their days of silence, and I smiled back. And sometimes Sister Theresa, in her yard near the clothesline, handed me a piece of candy or a glittering marble, as I walked back to Cottage Eleven after public school.

Perhaps this is why, today, I sometimes want to visit a convent, or even to live there, to study, to read, to work and to pray. Those sisters represented a kindly home for someone like me. Yet my pals, walking home after school, never knew too much about my friends at the nunnery.

They didn't need to pay attention or to imagine a life of God's love inside those silent gates behind the clothesline. Yet I found, somehow, a real yet imaginary refuge there. A billowing angelic presence. Visible yet invisible in the wind. Usually seen in the clear sky of a southern

California sun, yet one day, drenched in rain, with puddles of mud. Through the clouds.

One day I really did fly away. Clear across the USA, with my new family, the Robinsons. And finally, the reign of the children's home ended. Yet forever waving to me in memory.

After awhile the houseparents told us not to walk there anymore — that if we took a way home from school that was off the beaten path, private property and "don't get into trouble" — it was too dangerous. I missed those walks to that place! Maybe they thought we would be abducted by aliens.

A Place of Peace

During those years at Vista Del Mar my childhood visits, experiences and imaginings, including my wish that I could live in this small religious community, gave me a sense of God's love, security and trust that I didn't receive at all in any other place or way. In this realm, I was able to escape the coldness and the depersonalization I often felt at Vista.

I sensed another realm, a spiritual love, a concrete structure and the faces of the smiling nuns, the sunshine and the gardens, the image of the cross. I sensed an institution that seemed to me, at the time, a place of peace, a place of spiritual love. Perhaps that is the reason I have always enjoyed visiting the Catholic Church.

Flos Carmeli (Flower of Carmel)

13th-century hymn to Our Lady attributed
to Carmelite St. Simon Stock

Flower of Carmel, tall vine, blossom-laden;
splendour of heaven, child-bearing, yet maiden;
none equals thee.

Mother so tender, whom no man didst know,
on Carmel's children thy favors bestow;
Star of the Sea!

Strong stem of Jesse, who bore one bright flower,
be ever near us, and guard us each hour,
who serve thee here.

Purest of lilies, that flowers among thorns,
bring help to true hearts that in weakness turn
and trust in thee.

Strongest of armour, we trust in thy might,
under thy mantle, hard pressed in the fight,
we call to thee.

Our way, uncertain, surrounded by foes,
unfailing counsel you offer to those
who turn to thee.

O gentle Mother, who in Carmel reigns,
share with your servants that gladness you gained,
and now enjoy.

Hail, gate of heaven, with glory now crowned,
bring us to safety, where thy Son is found,
true joy to see.
Amen. (Alleluia.)

+ ***Flos Carmeli Prayer Note:*** Although everything in this collection is a combination of my childhood experience, in both memory and imagination, the convent story is the most fanciful. Thus I include the lovely Flos Carmeli prayer as a lasting, living tribute to the power of faith, prayer and imagination to see me through life.

The Early Seeds of Devotion

the sisters
I wanted to be like them

fragile yet strong
quietly humming in the garden

chanting in their cloister
chanting inside their gate
the gate with the large stone cross

where we once knocked
after school
to say hello

the nuns knew my story
perhaps they prayed for me

perhaps that is where
I find this love
this intrigue this Catholic mystery

this rich Catholic love
I cannot yet explain
and yet I know them

The Nunnery Near Vista, A Fragment

"We wear this hat and dress as our habit in the Carmelite Cloister."

"Like caramel candy?" I asked.

"We are called Carmelite nuns because we belong to a special place named Mount Carmel, where Jesus our Lord is remembered," she said.

"Hey, sister," said Stanley, a Cottage Eleven child who sometimes walked home with me, "Do you sisters have some Carmelite candy for Halloween?"

He was a smart kid who could never resist a witty comeback.

"Come by next time it's Halloween and we'll leave a surprise for you," said the sister.

Maybe, just maybe, the healing convent prayers and the brief exchanges of silence, whisper, chanting and voice helped me stay alive to myself at Vista.

At age eight or nine, I knew I wasn't of that faith. Yet in my heart, I think I really knew that was the perfect kind of place for me to live, to play, to love God, to commune with Him, to receive solace, help, comfort and love from nature.

a wave and a flower
even a chant
heard through the gate

peaceful secretive silent
living near Vista
the Carmelite nunnery

now I wish
we could have
stayed for afternoon tea
or even a lesson
on the Holy Rosary

a chance to learn
how to knit
and a glimpse of
the Mother Superior's wit

I wanted to live there
I wanted to see
inside the gate
the Holy See

Convent Time

one day walking 'home' after school
I found a new place
across the open field
of tall grass and wild flowers

a place new and out of the way
the Carmelite convent
mysterious castle of stone and story unknown

the white sheets on the swaying clothesline
the chanting Carmelite sisters
in the distance in sunlight

after that first visit
I saw them and sometimes heard them
behind closed doors praying
in the midst of their daily chores

in the many times of silence
when they couldn't answer me
I yet found a glimpse inside
the holy whisper the smile the wave

and in the gifts they gave to me
homemade candy fruit juice and devotion
my mysterious childhood is resurrected

today I pray the Rosary
along the roads of faith
in remembrance of secret places

A Quiet Balance

all of my life
I have been
wishing for this star

a natural sense
within me
searching for the way

some bright light
yet not too bright
a soft and gentle breeze
yet the wind
not too strong

a balance
between two extremes

finding my place
sharing that place of knowing

finding that purpose
searching with others

giving voice
to the quiet
voice within

through intuition
the magical harmony
repeats itself
until I no longer
hear the discord

a quiet balance emerges
against all odds

I can share
who I am
against all odds
a quiet balance emerges,
quiet remembrance.

"I am in the chapel"

For St. Teresa Benedicta of the Cross

I am in the chapel
even while the light is low
I am your Betrothed
your family and your friends

I am the papal message
the Hebrew mysteries
the Moroccan spiral

I am the host
the Lord of Lords
I am the silent vow
the mission the flaw the insight

I am today and always
now and forever
your keeper new and glorious
Amen

+ Born Edith Stein, (October 12, 1891–August 9, 1942), St. Teresa Benedicta of the Cross was a German Jewish philosopher who converted to Roman Catholicism and became a Discalced Carmelite nun. She is canonized as a martyr and saint of the Catholic Church. Her statue at St. Peter's Basilica in the Vatican shows her holding the Torah in one hand, a cross in the other hand.

IV. The Four Seasons

To those who had lost their way and had become desperate, the Master, through the disciple said:

"I will lead you through the dark night of the soul.
Give unto Me all your shortcomings.
I will lift you above them.
I am the ocean of Love.
You shall be redeemed.
You shall find my Peace."

—Meher Baba
(Through Norina Matchabelli)
Norina's Gift,
Christopher Wilson and
Charles Haynes

Spring

Passover — Crossing the Red Sea

During my first or second Passover at Vista Del Mar, the younger children started to receive special after-school tutoring sessions. We were learning to read parts of the Passover Seder celebration in Hebrew and some were also practicing in English. I was one of several of the best readers among our group in Cottage Eleven, and I was chosen to participate, for reading aloud part of the Four Questions.

The Four Questions are an integral aspect of the traditional Seder, the Passover meal that celebrates the Jewish people fleeing slavery in Egypt and traveling to freedom. Special holiday foods are served with wine and the liberation story is told during the meal.

For several weeks we practiced, receiving much needed and appreciated special attention, approval and encouragement from our tutors and housemothers. A special clothing allowance was supplied so we could get new outfits for the Passover dinner celebration. My birth mother was permitted to visit me to take me shopping for this event, although my parents would not be attending.

Little by little or maybe all at once, we children realized this event would really be a big deal, and we had to play our part. Some of the high-ranking officials from the board of a philanthropy organization would be attending this special Seder celebration.

That evening, the large gym at Vista, where the event took place, was decorated to look like an elegant banquet hall with festive tablecloths, dishes, silverware and flowers. The bright and dazzling lights looked so different to me. Perhaps the unique lights were especially decorated to look like chandeliers for that evening. Maybe I imagined this different sense of light.

For several weeks beforehand, there were vague and uncertain rumors among the children and our housemothers that the financial status and upkeep of the home might directly benefit from our recital of the Four Questions.

When I heard these rumors, I felt strange, ambivalent, eager to please, eager to meet the important guests, wanting to do a good deed that would help the home. Yet inside, I felt a deep emptiness, a sense that I was invisible — not seen for myself, only a symbol of a young girl at the home who could please the guests and maybe they would smile and like me. Perhaps I secretly wished that someone there, one of them, would become my special friend.

That Passover evening, I observed the guests of honor who were seated at a special, separate table. To me, as a child in need of love and attention, these visitors seemed to be people who cared more about the finances and the smooth day-to-day operation of the institution than about nurturing the individual children. Even as a small child, I strongly sensed a coldness from those guests, an impersonal encounter that nevertheless seemed so important. Yet I felt empty inside.

Perhaps that night was when I became a poet, a prophet. The night that as the Four Questions states, is "...different from all other nights..." Today I am a victor who may explore a tragedy and find there a story to gift to others. Perhaps that evening is when I discovered I wasn't alone in my search for freedom — that my yearning for love and freedom was also the yearning of the world and of the other children. And perhaps, in a way, this was the beginning of my sense of self in relationship to others.

After we recited the Four Questions (with at least one small child even needing to stand on a chair to be seen) and the Seder service ended, the glow I had felt inside, the anticipation, the extra attention from housemothers and tutors completely vanished. We went back to our substandard food, broken hopes and day to day institutional indifference.

Today I know that except for a few kind social workers, an exceptional houseparent and occasional volunteers, we were surrounded by people who were just getting by, doing their jobs, with little training, education or understanding for how to relate to us.

As a young child I naturally wanted to be loved everyday for myself, not only for doing certain chores (or religious ceremonies) in a pleasing way, to improve efficiency at the home. In my empathy for others now, I sense a connection between the years I lived at Vista and the lack of love, understanding and compassion that I saw all around me, that I felt all the time there.

I slowly found God at the Jewish Children's Home, as I prayed and spoke to Him, pleading to be able to see my family, pleading to be released from that cold, heartless institution. Eventually, my prayers were answered.

This afternoon as I was taking a nap, I suddenly had an image of a small open boat floating out in the middle of the sea. I was in the boat, along with the other children from Cottage Eleven. Perhaps as a young reader of the Four Questions at the Passover Seder that evening, I imagined that we would all one day be able to cross the Red Sea into freedom, which is the meaning of the celebration for Passover.

Orphanage Heart Healing

learning to chant the Passover Four Questions
in a holy yet unholy minor key

how lovely I thought at age eight or nine
finally someone is paying attention to me

even a special class in Hebrew
and a few in private tutorial

when on the first night of Passover
I discovered or maybe imagined
this was done only for show

to impress donors idealists philanthropists
visiting to fund the Jewish children's home

I carry this memory still
in every fiber of my being
how can a small child understand

except perhaps in the heart of no division
no brick walls no old postcards no war
no dread now or ever

+ At the traditional Seder meal for Passover, as part of the liturgy during the feast, the Four Questions are typically asked by a child or the youngest person.

Summer

Camp Saratoga

This evening I found some photographs of me with other children at the two children's homes where I spent several years of my childhood.

In the summer of 1960, Ruth and Rabbi Michael A. Robinson, the Jewish family that I visited on weekends in Pomona, California, arranged and paid for me to attend a summer camp, away from the David and Margaret Children's Home in La Verne.

I believe some of the other children at this camp also had experienced family difficulties. I only found that out when I arrived at camp, while waiting in line, when a child next to me shared that this was a camp for "kids with family problems."

The chance to go to camp was supposed to make me feel happy yet I was not too enthusiastic at first. Some of the people were kind and understanding. Swimming in a lake was fun, horseback riding was rather strange.

I still remember that I felt uncomfortable learning to ride a horse, and especially how I accidentally held the reins too tight during our first group horseback ride on the trails. I knew that I was doing my best to follow the instructions of the counselor who taught horseback riding. Yet I was also very nervous and didn't understand everything that she was saying. The ride was not going well for me. I finally was able to get the counselor to see that the horse's mouth was bleeding. After that incident and for the entire camp session, I felt that this counselor was not interested in me. Perhaps because I did not learn as quickly as she wished, and I also felt that there was a feeling of regimentation in her behavior which did not suit my sensitive self. I had done my best to follow her instructions. I see now that for much of my entire adult life, I have lived with this memory and that it has impacted the way I am able to learn.

Ping pong was fun and I liked the hikes. One of the boys was partially blind and had a caregiver with him. He walked with a cane.

I liked him especially yet was not able to spend much time with him.

Getting to read books anytime I wanted to was helpful. I had a small Polaroid camera, too. In this summer camp photograph I look happy, with my arm around another girl.

When the camp was over, we were taken to a central location to wait for our rides home. While the other children were met immediately, with loving greetings from parents and siblings, after some discussion I realized there was no one there to take me back to the children's home.

After waiting for some time, thinking they were just late, I managed to borrow a dime and received help from one of the counselors. We phoned the Robinsons and they somehow arranged to contact the David and Margaret Children's Home.

Since there was no one available there to drive to the area where I was waiting, a camp supervisor was kind enough to drive me back to the David and Margaret Home. I had a late Sunday supper, grateful to have been able to get a ride and to not be lost forever.

No one had even thought to arrange a ride home for me.

Autumn

The Candy Apple

I believe this story is from my first Halloween at Vista Del Mar Children's Home, when I was seven years old.

During the holidays, the Campfire Girls and other places donated a lot of sweets and small handmade gifts for the children and teenagers at Vista. So for once, during lunchtime, we were given something special that the other children in public school envied.

In our schoolyard, another child I had never seen before was eagerly watching me begin to eat the caramel-coated candy apple, after I had finally unwrapped the sticky paper. He offered me a few pennies, maybe even five cents, so he could have the candy apple. His wide eyes seemed to be pleading.

I immediately gave the candy apple to him. I hardly had a chance to taste it. I didn't even have a single bite. I felt deeply sorry for him in my child-sensitive self. Perhaps I was hoping he would be my friend.

I felt shy and envious as I then saw the little boy look at me one last time before he began eating the apple and then quickly going to play elsewhere. I don't even remember if I had a chance to get the little bit of money he offered me. I was so eager to make him happy.

I suppose life is always
a mysterious exchange
of gifts blessings and the unknown

Thanksgiving for Vista Del Mar

if this is a gift
get me out of this rift

a dose of PTSD
enough for three
yet at that place

no Trinity
the best is yet to be
for a special life lift

alone on Sundays mostly
except for a friend
who was really a hood
in that old neighborhood

of traumatized children
housemothers therapists
and rotten food
yet I see the good
one needs to always

like the voice of God
like the childish prayers
I believe they finally
led me elsewhere

from home to home
and then at last
to Him, the Lord of whim.

Winter

One Little Light

Christmas at the Jewish Children's Home was a Hanukah candle that I never got to light. The privilege went to the oldest and baddest kid, Arthur. Although forever, for weeks, I was promised I never had the chance.

now I see or remember
a safety issue
the housemother was told
not to let us young ones
be so bold with candles

a bunch of rowdy kids
not so cool to light the non-Yule

oy vey
what a mixed up time and memory
for a magical holiday

now everyday is a holiday
when I am with you
Great Spirit Holy One
Abba Jesus the Comforter

Christmas and Hanukah both are shared, sacred, special
to me and my identity.

For the Holidays

Because, as a young child, I couldn't have regular visits with my birth parents, the holidays were lonely. I can recall receiving a few Hanukah and birthday gifts from my birth parents, and opening them in the meeting area in Cottage Eleven, by myself, while other children were out with their families.

One special time, Evelyn Rudie, the child actress, was included in a special star performance that was given for us kids at Vista, along with Hollywood actors Jeff Chandler and Mel Blanc. Around 1959. I think she was introduced as having run away and then coming home.

Years later, when I was back in Santa Monica, I saw a notice about the Santa Monica Playhouse that mentioned her as playwright and director. I took a bus there and saw her performance. She still manages that theatre group, creating and acting in plays for children.

I think I was too shy at the time to introduce myself many years ago, when I visited her theatre. The episode in her life of running away as a child was also traumatic for her, so I think that was another reason I didn't introduce myself, so as not to draw her back to that time in her life. I wish I had met her again.

"I hold the white jade"

I hold the white jade
there is beauty
on the stone path

I love the beauty
on the stone path

V. Visits No Visits

We must lose ourselves in order to find ourselves.
Thus loss itself is gain.

— Meher Baba, *God Speaks*

Visits or Not

At Vista, I never fully understood why I couldn't see my folks on Sundays, like the other kids my age in Cottage Eleven, who were allowed to go home on Sundays and holiday weekends.

When I first arrived at Vista, there were months of separation, suspense, court decisions and my tears, until finally, once a month alternating weekday visits were granted to my birth parents, brief visits for several years during the rest of my stay at Vista.

During holidays when the other children were on weekend visits with their parents, my birth father received permission to send a check to Mrs. Katz, to take me, with child residents Susie and Maurice, to a restaurant or to an extra film. And on Valentine's Day, he sent a large heart-shaped box of chocolates that Mrs. Katz kept in her room and shared with me and the other children.

Life continued this way until my move to the Methodist David and Margaret Home, where life was better, and there, my birth parents were permitted to visit me for three hours each alternate Sunday, on the spacious grounds of the home, alongside the other children and teenagers whose parents had the same visitation time.

Post Watch with Holly

how with this rage shall beauty hold a plea, whose action is no stronger than a flower

— William Shakespeare

today and in my memory
the outdoor sage blossoms
yet she needs no water
and there is very little sunshine
"drought resistant" my friend Jane tells me

while writing birthday thank you notes
I found myself floundering
remembering myself, a young child
given permission for writing
thank you birthday notes
holiday thank you greetings to my family

in the Jewish Children's Home
while completely removed for weeks months years
denied visiting times
with some later exceptions and brief moments

I dance in this memory
in forgiveness and surreal connection

knowing that finished letters
now have a place
and a sense of recognition
through His love and Grace

knowing this now
that sometimes a poem
for family and friends enters my heart
and I may reach out to speak
and there are those who will see me.

+ Holly is a Bach Flower remedy.

Tikkun Olam

A belief and a sense of determination that someday I could be able to leave Vista Del Mar Children's Home and to live in a better place kept me going. This faith and belief in finding freedom still influences my life today. My specific childhood experiences using prayer and having a sense of compassion for the suffering of the other traumatized children at Vista Del Mar planted the seeds for my outlook as an adult.

to mend the thread
of the universe
found and holy
tikkun olam

+ Tikkun Olam is a Hebrew phrase — to heal, to repair, to restore the world.

A Time of Insight

Today the wild rose gives me comfort. Even in your thorns there is a touch of remorse, and a sense of comfort. The wind sings your praise this early spring day, as the cyclamen comes back to life in gentle green renewal.

The piano keys touch my heart in their notes reclaimed, in the hands of remembrance and in my life, I sing your praise.

+ Listening to Variations Serieuses in D Minor by Felix Mendelssohn on my radio.

A Thread of Gold

morning mist a light went on inside me
somewhere to walk after work
someone to visit
tea brandy scones

in the back of the church social hall
a new yet old visitor
an offer of friendship

the light lessens my sad memory
early years in two children's homes
the disappointment when school is out
and no one is around to pay attention

except we children played together outdoors
and I sometimes sat in the lodge
watching "I Led Three Lives"
the "Loretta Young Show" on TV
and "The Millionaire"

watching and listening also
in the light open lodge
the teenagers dance
playing the vinyl records
"See You In September"
"Silhouettes On The Shade"
that's how I know these songs

once I asked Mrs. Miller, housemother
"What's a communist?"
she hesitated then "Someone who is different."
so I thought that was me too
as an exception to the rule

a social worker visiting with me once a week
said, "That answer is not the whole story."

Loretta Young, "The Millionaire" actor and Queen Elizabeth
became my imaginary family
in this surreal portrait of my childhood
my buried treasure now, forever perhaps.

+ Marvin Miller was the actor in "The Millionaire."

In the Children's Home
(A Remembrance)

my little closet
in Cottage Eleven
what treasures I hid

inside a small drawer
a single dime
and the candy
from the corner store

and free Tootsie Roll Pops
from the place nearby
where they made them
gifts from the factory work crew

these little pursuits
a child's vision of heaven

and maybe a letter written backwards
on a secret scrap of paper
a letter lost in the wind
or tossed into the autumn bonfire
sometimes around Halloween

here is a toast
to the motley crew
of orphaned kids
and houseparents too
and the karma brew
that created the stew.

"prayers of forgiveness"

prayers of forgiveness
and the soul of a witness
etched in my coloring book
hidden under the bed
memory of Vista
child's scrapbook of memory

I Wanted to Die

One day after school, maybe when a once again planned parental visit never happened, I laid down on the street near cars driving by the Vista Del Mar office. I was near where the social worker could see me. I was eight years old or so.

I know that I needed to express the depth of my despair. I don't remember what they did, except to tell me to stand up and to get out of the way of the cars. When I went to dinner that night with the other children and the houseparents, there was a feeling of shame and "Oh, she just wants attention."

After that, I saw the psychiatrist more often. Dr. Miller was calm and detached when he asked me what had happened. "Maybe you just wanted someone to see you," he said, "Someone who could give you more attention."

"I wanted to die," I said.

After that they let me see my parents from time to time, making sure the visits were a little more frequent and clearly defined.

The Vista Psychiatrist

Somehow my father found out the day of Dr. Miller's birthday, and I was sent a gift to give to Dr. Miller from us. Dr. Miller was surprised. A blue tie and a box of chocolates.

I deeply regretted seeing Dr. Miller when the other kids were able to play outside or make arts and crafts after school in a special program during the same time as my appointments with him.

I was supposed to see him once a week. Sometimes I skipped the sessions. He never colored with me, only analyzed my drawings. I think I made sad looking drawings just to interest him and get him to comment. Now I can appreciate the way he sympathetically agreed with me about another troubled girl. And how his counseling times with me may have been somewhat limited and placed on observation. Perhaps that is why I recall the feeling of vague discomfort during some of our sessions.

One day I received a typewritten note at public school, letting me know I needed to keep my appointments with Dr. Miller each Wednesday afternoon. Reminding me, as if I had forgotten! The note seemed to me to be a mix of mystery, special attention, disappointment and relief that at least I wasn't being publicly admonished. The letter seems to have given me a sense of importance. When I misbehaved or didn't follow a rule, at least someone noticed me. I still recall the sense of receiving a letter, sealed in an envelope, as letters from both parents were often not permitted.

Orphan Talisman

the heart shaped stone
has a special place
on your throne

I hold onto this stone
when I am alone
like you once asked me to
my Beloved

on the night of a blue moon
when Ronnie cried
or someone lied
you were there by my side

when a kid was mean
or acted obscene
you held on to my scream

then my loss
became years later
your dream

my imagination and my search
my purpose and potential
all are alive within those stones of spirit

rejoicing waiting to be found
grieving waiting to be loved
waiting to love you
in their secret way prasad

Imagination in Isolation

On Saturday, after lunch, the young children in Cottage Eleven were driven to the local cinema. The films were free for us, and we went there almost every weekend except on the rare occasions when a film was considered unsuitable. Or when we were driven to Knott's Berry Farm or to the Santa Monica beach on special occasions by a volunteer. Later, we also visited Disneyland. I always preferred Knott's Berry Farm, the place seemed more old-fashioned with a quietness that evoked a more serene childhood landscape.

In the dining room at Cottage Eleven, I remember there were several rows of locked cabinets. On Saturdays, the housemother on duty that day would open the cabinets. There was a separate shelf or tray of candy for each of the two dozen or so children. We were each given one or two handfuls of candy, in a small sack. These we could take to the cinema.

Mrs. T was in charge of the storeroom down the road at the children's home. When the candy supply was low one of the children would walk down to give Mrs. T the message, and the list of supplies that were needed. I was sometimes given the lucky chore. I enjoyed seeing Mrs. T, sometimes getting a sample of candy. Mrs. T was also a storyteller.

We children saved some of our Halloween candy to put into the cabinets, so that we had a once a week Saturday portion as a treat. Halloween was the only time I saw the inside of a "real" home during my two and a half years in the Jewish children's home. Volunteers would invite us into their houses for Halloween visits and refreshments.

On Sundays, most of the other children were away from the children's home. They were visiting their families. I did not go home to my family. After school or on weekends when I was sitting alone at the outdoor social picnic area, I would watch the cars drive over the highway bridge, in the distance. I would imagine that my birth mother was driving to see me.

Sundays at the Children's Home

Little by little I remember what happened during the two and one half years of Sundays at the Vista Del Mar Jewish Children's Home.

Each Sunday most of the young children I lived with in Cottage Eleven went to visit their parents and other relatives. A few of us didn't get to see our families.

I didn't mind being alone after awhile, although I never knew for sure when I would get to see my family. I was assigned special and different visiting hours, getting to see my mother once a month on the premises of the home, for ten minutes, then lengthened to thirty minutes.

For the first three months there, I didn't see her at all. There was always an uncertainty as to how much time I would have and whether I could see her and my father.

Because of my deepening unhappiness in this situation, I began to earnestly speak to God, praying and talking with Him when I was seven years old. I spoke with Him inwardly, at first silently and later, sometimes speaking out loud and listening. A few other children and houseparents sometimes heard me "talking to myself." When that happened, I would be silent or whisper to myself and be more careful.

Then I somehow adjusted to reading alone in the outdoor pavilion, books available from the cottage like Nancy Drew, Cherry Ames and the Hardy Boys, or watching television in the lodge and occasionally getting to hang out with a couple of older teenage girls. For various reasons, they also did not have a family place to go on Sundays.

One of these girls, Maxine, was very intimidating. She warned me not to tell if I saw the girls doing something "wrong." I liked her, even though I may have also been afraid of her. Maybe because we were both all alone, without parents. Even as a young child with my own trouble, I sensed a sadness in Maxine, although she appeared to be rebellious and outwardly acted tough.

In my aloneness, I withdrew to God in prayer. Maxine was more likely to act intimidating or to be mischievous. Yet seeing Maxine on a Sunday was bound to be an adventure, if she could get away with what she wanted to do. I still recall her walking toward me when I would see her during our free time on Sundays. She would smile when she saw me walking around by myself "up in the home," then act like she didn't care or didn't need to speak with me, then soon became friendly again, inviting me to participate in a secret and hidden adventure that she and several of the other teenage girls were carefully planning.

Once after the girls collected a few cigarette butts they decided to see about pooling their spare change to buy a packet of cigarettes. They asked me if I would like something, too, because, "You are too young to smoke cigarettes, right?" I agreed, I had no desire to smoke.

One girl, Veronica, planted flowers in the cottages "up in the home" where the older teenage girls and boys lived. I liked her. The other three girls, Michelle, Maxine and Naomi let me spend time with them. They tried on lipstick, painted their finger nails, and listened to programs on a transistor radio. We sometimes had money for soda pop, too.

When Naomi returned with the cigarettes, the girls warned me not to say a word to the housemother when I got back to Cottage Eleven for dinner that evening. They gave me some mint chewing gum and a small bag of red hot cinnamon candy. They kept gum for themselves as well, to hide the tobacco scent.

"Well, what will you do if I tell?" I asked Maxine. "You aren't supposed to do this. They said so."

"Girl, if you say a word I will twist your arm off," said Maxine, as she lit a fresh cigarette.

Later that day, when I got back to Cottage Eleven for a snack, the housemother asked me how my visit with the girls turned out. I must have had a guilty look on my face. She asked me what we did, over and over and over. I said we danced in the lodge, saw Veronica planting flowers and that they gave me red hot cinnamon candy and some mint chewing gum. Of course she wanted some of the candy, too.

The mint chewing gum must have tipped off Mrs. Katz, my housemother. She somehow got me to admit that the girls had been smoking cigarettes in secret. She then told the housemother in charge of the teenage girls and they were punished with a brief curfew concerning leaving the home on their own.

When Maxine next saw me, she seized my arm and twisted it. Then she said, "I bet that Mrs. Katz made you confess! Sorry I twisted your arm. Hope you aren't hurt too bad. Want another piece of mint chewing gum?"

When I next had an appointment with the home psychiatrist, Dr. Miller, I complained to him about Maxine, and then said I felt sorry for her. Dr. Miller agreed with me. Maxine was a troubled and unhappy looking girl. "Sometimes unhappy people hurt one another and they do so because of their own unhappiness," he said. Dr. Miller reassured me that I was not to blame when the teenage girls were discovered with cigarettes. He smiled at me and asked me if maybe I secretly admired Maxine. I said that maybe I did. He seemed happy that I finally agreed with one of his comments or interpretations.

My father was concerned about the level of neglect and lack of attention I experienced on Sundays when the other children went to their families. He became friends with another dad, and found out I was all alone on Sundays.

After my birth father began to complain to local judges, law givers, the director of the home, and even wrote to politicians about the neglect that I was suffering, the home made some efforts to improve my situation.

A Big Sister was assigned to take me on Sunday outings as well, when the other kids were with their parents. She was a young woman with an automobile and we went for a drive to a park and had some refreshments. However, the visit was rather brief, and I still had to go back to the home before the other children returned in the early evening from visits with their families.

I recall a deep sense of sadness when she was unable to visit with me after only a few special times. There was a problem somewhere, a bureaucratic mix-up, lack of funding, complaints from someone somewhere regarding my visits with her. Perhaps a disagreement between my parents ended those happy times.

Shortly after my brief visits with the Big Sister, the staff social worker I really loved had a special meeting with me. She spoke gently with me, letting me know that because my father had complained so much, I would have to leave Vista.

I would soon be visiting a new place, in La Verne, California, where I would be the only Jewish child. She was sorry I had to leave. She said soon a probation office from the department of social services would take me to the new place in La Verne for a tour and to meet the other children. When we got to the Methodist place, the David and Margaret Home, it was around the time of the Christmas school vacations.

So most of the other children at Vista were having an overnight holiday visit with their families. Yet even though appropriate arrangements had been made and the staff in La Verne were expecting us, when we arrived, all I could do was walk around the place and meet the handyman, because all of the children, for the school holiday, were up in the mountains seeing the snow.

Such were the institutional challenges facing me and the children's home from time to time. When I finally, with relief and satisfaction, at the age of ten, left Vista Del Mar to live at the David and Margaret Home, I was gifted with a delightful and wonderful children's book, "The Earth for Sam." Part of a trilogy from the Cottage Eleven book shelf. There was also "The Sea for Sam" and "The Stars for Sam."

That book is about geology, and now I see, also a symbol of Meher Baba's ocean of love for my life and meeting with my future adoptive parents, Ruth and Rabbi Michael A. Robinson. I met them soon after moving into the David and Margaret Home, thanks to my birth father's efforts.

Visits No Visits

After my birth father had spoken and written to various officials, complaining of my predicament at Vista Del Mar, I was informed by the social worker at Vista that I would be transferred to the David and Margaret Home. I was glad to leave Vista, where I had lived for two and a half years, praying and pleading with God nearly every day to be released from that environment. Toward the end of my stay at Vista, I was finally permitted to spend a Sunday away from Vista with my birth mother and her family, a regular visiting schedule that nearly all of the other children in Cottage Eleven experienced, something that I had been denied during my life there.

This one time home visit was during the Christmas holiday season. For nearly two and one half years I had not seen my aunt or my grandmother. Except for two short and unexpected times. Once, from their car, my mother, aunt and grandmother unexpectedly and furtively waved to me while I was going home to Vista from public school. I was walking near the neighboring Catholic convent, in a secluded rural area that was my special path to walk after school. The second unexpected visit happened when they somehow knew the children from Vista would be visiting the Ocean Park Beach, to see the new Pacific Ocean Park. I was happy to see my family at the beach, yet recall being questioned afterward, when the housemother seemed to know I had secretly seen them.

Shortly after that rare Christmastime visit, at the age of ten, I was transferred to a Methodist children's home in La Verne, California. There, I was the only Jewish child. At the nearby Reform temple where I attended Sunday school, I met Rabbi Michael and Ruth Robinson. Soon they invited me to visit with them and their two young children on the weekends. When they were preparing to move to the east coast, they received permission to let me live with them as their foster child.

In the summer of 1960, I moved with the Robinson family to Croton-on-Hudson, New York. At the age of ten, living in Croton-on-Hudson, New York, I had a new life, a place of new potential. New clothes, good food, changes in language, environment, people, values, new aunts, uncles and cousins, even a new last name! When I was twelve, Ruth and Michael Robinson were able to adopt me.

For my own life, becoming part of a new family at age ten gives me, even now, a subtle sense of connection to people I know who have experienced upheavals in their lives, including people who have emigrated from one country to another.

A Letter Never Mailed

They assailed me on my day of disaster,
but Yahweh was my support;
he freed me, set me at large,
he rescued me, since he loves me.

— Psalm 18:18–19
The Jerusalem Bible

At Vista Del Mar I missed my birth mother so much that I thought I would die. After several weeks at the children's home, I finally realized, to my child mind, that maybe I would never see my mommy again.

Due to the difficult family circumstances and the resulting home atmosphere, the courts and Department of Social Services placed me in Vista Del Mar Children's Home with no parental visits. I only realized this shock after the first few weeks, as up to that time, I believed that my situation was like some children who went to sleep-away camp in the summer. Also, initially, no letters were permitted, no phone calls.

Once I knew what was happening, in my child-like scribble at the age of seven, I secretly wrote a letter to my mother saying that I missed her and that, "If they don't let me see you then I will run away." Some of the older children actually did run away, and maybe even the younger ones. I think that is how I got the idea.

At Vista Del Mar there was an office building where the kids would have scheduled appointments with therapists. After I had sealed the letter and written what I recalled to be my mother's address, I paid whatever pennies I had to the receptionist for a postage stamp. Around that time I was scheduled for an appointment with my social worker.

In my utter innocence I politely asked the receptionist for help to mail the letter. Since it was time for my appointment, she promised to make sure that I had written the correct address on the envelope. The letter, having been supposedly placed in the office mailbox for outgoing mail, was intercepted by someone in the office, and I was "found out breaking the rules of no family letters."

I recall a houseparent or other persons in charge making comments at the time, saying with sarcasm and confidence, even arrogance, that they were sure I had wanted to be caught anyhow. That I was trying to get some extra attention so people would feel sorry for me. So people would have pity on "poor little Sharon."

I was only seven years old and had been placed at Vista with no family communication or visits. I recall a sense of shame and guilt that I had wanted to find my mother. In the outdoor patio, near our after-school play area, I began to watch the cars driving along the Los Angeles freeway in the distance, imagining I could see her car passing by, and that I still remembered what her car looked like. Perhaps my imagination at this time is what saved me from total emotional and mental collapse.

Soon after, I was placed in weekly psychiatric sessions with Dr. Miller. I had bonded with the gentle, compassionate social worker, yet was told "my case" was too complicated and I had "more problems" than the social worker could be expected to handle.

Dr. Miller was not a warm or friendly person, he needed to be highly observant and he refused to "make art" with me. I would do almost anything, make up any excuse to avoid my appointments with him.

I can still recall coming back to Cottage Eleven from a session with Dr. Miller. All the other children had been given an arts and crafts class in a special art studio next to our living quarters. I was able to see some of their finished projects, including oranges with cloves in them to make designs. I was heart-broken that I hadn't been there. "Those spiced orange pomander balls were fun to make," one of the kids told me. "How come you couldn't be here to join us? Don't you like to make art with us?"

Eventually the Los Angeles court permitted me to see my birth mother on a very limited basis, and then, also, my birth father. After that, my birth father would mysteriously find out the date of Dr.

Miller's birthday, and give me birthday presents as well as Christmas gifts to give to Dr. Miller during my counseling sessions. I believe he was very grateful for Dr. Miller in my life.

I was also finally allowed to receive letters. I recall that my family phone calls were generally still restricted, a rule that definitely deprived me of choice conversations that were allowed to the other children, however brief, on a weekly basis, from the hallway payphone in Cottage Eleven.

Something about not wanting me to hear or to say anything that would upset me. Too much for the housemothers to take on, as they were limited without the professional knowledge or insight for knowing how to cope with such an episode on a school night.

Once I received an important message that my birth father would be on television, one of several attempts he made to publicize my unfortunate situation. Then I was told he would be on the radio instead. In the topsy-turvy world of housemother rumors, gossip and secrecy, he would occasionally give the main housemother presents, and thus I was told I could see the television show. However, again in that disjointed world, the time and day of the interview he was having to plead for me and to tell his side of the family story was incorrect. Moreover, I sense the housemother, Anna Katz, feared for her job if she dared "take sides" or allow me to hear such a program.

I recall a single brief and unfamiliar television image, perhaps not a good reception, and voices on the radio that I had difficulty recognizing. Perhaps this "getting the wrong time or night for the program" was the housemother's way of accepting a gift, placating my father, and neutralizing the situation. No doubt she was in a difficult situation, in a place where she was probably rarely given gifts, as far as I know.

My birth father, an Orthodox Jew who was a capmaker in his small family shop while I was growing up and who later became a successful businessman, is clearly the hero of this disturbing tragedy. His letters to southern California government officials and judges complaining of the conditions at Vista Del Mar Jewish Children's Home finally resulted in my release to a better place in La Verne, California; a Methodist children's home with a farm, where I thrived.

Years later, at the second place, I met and was eventually adopted by the Robinson family, also with my birth father's encouragement.

I have done my best to pursue the truth about what happened to me in my family situation as a child and at Vista Del Mar. As an adult, I requested and I received a copy of my records from Vista Del Mar Children's Home, clarifying some of the issues in my life there. Yet ultimately, these stories are my memories and perceptions of my life and of the time I spent in the children's home, the way I experienced the trauma of this experience and the need to share these stories with others.

Mrs. T from the Children's Home

Mrs. T came to see me today
she was hiding behind a silk screen
in the candy section of the supply room

where I would visit
or bring over a message
from the housemother in Cottage Eleven

usually asking Mrs. T
for more of this or that
delivered in her truck
down the hill to our place

today Mrs. T came to see me
she reminds me to visit
a friend at the end of the day
an imaginary person or real

even to pray the hours
in a made up version of life
this silent walking time.

Marilyn

This morning, after visiting my neighbor Port Townsend neighbor, Maureen, and stringing beads with her to repair some bracelets and necklaces, I wistfully said goodbye. She showed me the tree across the street, and cautioned me to be careful. "Something needs to be done so no one walks into it at night," she said. "See you in church."

In some ways, I admire Maureen's family life. Visits with grandchildren who play at her place once a week, cards on the weekends with her mom, the local Elks club dances with her husband, and her commitment as a member of St. Paul's Episcopal Church Altar Guild.

I realized that I missed having a big sister; that was somehow the way I perceived my neighborly friendship with Maureen. To my surprise, I remembered my friend Marilyn in Vista Del Mar Children's Home.

Marilyn was an older girl in Cottage Eleven. She would comfort me and listen to me when I missed seeing my family. She came into my side of the girl's dormitory room one day, smiling mysteriously. Marilyn told me that finally she was going to be leaving Vista.

She had always encouraged me to pray for my wish to see my family, my wish to live in a better place. I knew I would miss Marilyn. "I will see you again," she said as she walked away, getting ready to pack her suitcase. When a child who was well-loved was leaving Vista, there was always a sense of relief and also, sadness.

"Maurice is such a sweet and lovable child," mused Audrey, one of the housemothers. "I am happy to see he is going to a good home."

Said as a comment to me and Susie, the two girls who didn't have families to go home to — visits weren't allowed. Maurice is one of the lucky ones, I thought to myself. Would Susie or I ever have the chance to live in a family again? When Susie left Vista later on, to be placed in a foster home, there was little regret. She was both a sometime bully and a victim of the group of boys in Cottage Eleven who teased some of the girls.

One day I was in my side of the girl's dormitory when Marilyn, now a visitor, found me. "I was hoping to see you," she said. "I brought you a present." She handed me a small box and a card. A Valentine! On the card she had written, "For Sharon, a friendship ring."

The ring was turquoise blue, with a gold band. Marilyn, who was now a teenager, wore cool looking clothes and jewelry and she had a new hairdo.

"Are you happy?" I asked her. And we walked toward the dining hall for after school snacks.

"Yes," she whispered. "And I have a boyfriend. He gave this to me." Marilyn wore a gold heart-shaped locket around her neck. "We're going steady."

"I feel sorry for the kids who still live here," she said. That's one of the reasons I want to let you know that maybe after I finish high school and go to college, I can start a foster home for girls."

"I hope so, too," I said.

"today"

today
I can honestly say
with a mixture
of sadness and disbelief
I miss those kids

the jokes we played
the sadness of our stay
the games the gardens
the stories of childhood passage
at Vista Del Mar Children's Home

Disbelief because I never ever dreamed I would ever miss that part of my childhood. I feel that those years are no longer lost, they are replaced by a sense of love, with memories now experienced through a new life in Meher Baba.

VI. Where To? (Lost and Found)

I am the joy in your heart and the despair of your mind—for love can attain that which the intellect cannot fathom.

— Meher Baba,
Meher Baba Calling, p. 94

Looking Out

One day I had a vision of myself as a child and she said, "Please put me into a book."

Looking out on the freeway, hoping to catch a glimpse of my mother. Watching the filming in 1958 of "The Gift of Love" at Vista. Reading the Nancy Drew mysteries and "The Sea for Sam" book. I often wished that someday, someone would tell my story, too.

I always wondered where the trains were going. It was in the late 1950s. I was living at Vista Del Mar Children's Home. We had to walk near the train tracks everyday to go to school. The trains were a mystery. An escape, a potential refuge, shelter from the home that I lived in that wasn't really my home.

Quiet times of reading and silence were a refuge for me at Vista Del Mar Children's Home. Some of my favorite books were the Nancy Drew mystery stories, which were collected in the living room bookshelf in Cottage Eleven, where the younger children lived, and where I stayed as well.

A Television Show

As a young child living in Vista Del Mar one of my favorite television shows was *I Led Three Lives*, about the life of an FBI spy/communist agent/counter spy. I was very intrigued with this program and to this day, I love mysteries. One day, I asked one of my houseparents at the California children's home where I was living, "Mrs. Miller, what is a communist?" She looked perplexed. After some hesitation, and seeming to be an adult who needed to have an answer, she said, "Oh, a communist...that is someone who is different...different than us."

I suppose I was intrigued forever, since I am different.

Reading with a Flashlight

At Vista Del Mar there was a bookshelf in the children's lounge. The shelf had Nancy Drew mystery stories, the Hardy Boys and Cherry Ames nurse mysteries. The larger science books by William Maxwell Reed were also on the shelf, such as *The Sea for Sam*. I was able to develop my imagination in reading these books, even if I didn't understand all of the words.

I would sometimes sit in the children's lounge after school and on weekends, when the other kids were with their families. I would explore the different titles. No one else seemed to have an interest in these books. On weekdays after school, the other children went out to play near the large outdoor patio area and the teen lodge, where there was a playground.

I now realize that of course when the other kids went home on Sundays and holiday weekends to be with their families, they had their own books and toys and parents to guide them in their reading. They even had the chance to visit with family pets.

The housemothers encouraged me to go outside to play as well. In the evenings after dinner and kitchen chores, as we all sat in the living room lounge, boys and girls together, the housemother would often ask Arthur to play his guitar and to sing. When he finished, she would turn on the television.

I was more drawn to the bookshelves, including a set of encyclopedias that I discovered were located in a separate place at the far end of the living room, near our individual lockers.

I tried to put Kleenex into my ears so I would be able to have quiet time to read. Yet sitting in a corner table with a chosen book, in my separate, imaginary world, with Kleenex in my ears, was perceived as a threat to the normal evening routine. The housemother reported my behavior to the social worker!

My way out of this was to secretly read in bed at night when the other three or four girls in my dormitory room were sleeping. My birth father had given me a flashlight for my birthday. So at night, I would hide with my mystery book and my flashlight, under the covers.

Perhaps someone "told" on me, for I was warned that I had been discovered reading by flashlight at night in bed. I was told that if I continued to break the rules, I would have my "reading privileges" taken away. I solemnly promised never to do this again.

However, I think one housemother spoke to another and they were aware and watching to see and to "spy" on me. Since I was reading mysteries and watching reruns in the teenage lodge of the Cold War television show "I Led Three Lives," I already knew all about spies!

One evening, I heard the door to the bedroom open very quietly and slowly. Before this, I had been able to turn the flashlight off and hide my book when I heard a housemother's footsteps. This time, Anna Katz was wearing silent slippers. I didn't hear her walking down the hall. When she caught me she slapped my wrist, grabbed my flashlight and the Nancy Drew mystery book, "The Clue in the Diary" was taken away.

After that, I was sometimes allowed to take a book from the children's lounge and read outdoors, near the play area. I always felt the housemothers were judging me for my interest in books, as if they were suspicious of my personality, as if I were being subversive by my finding a miraculous way to survive my damaged childhood.

However, since some of the other children got into even worse trouble, behaving badly, getting into fights, playing tricks as kids do, yelling, teasing, name calling, stealing from each other, we all sort of bonded together in our dissatisfaction with the place.

Yet in recalling my early years there, I regret there was no one to encourage my love of books, a love which seemed to stay strong inside me. The housemothers, the rulemakers, those who merely tolerated my enthusiasm for literature could not break my spirit.

When I left Vista I lovingly said goodbye to the special bookshelf in our lounge — thankful for that one special place in the entire institution where I had learned and received comfort, solace and some of the very first literary experiences of my life.

After two and a half years at Vista, at the age of ten I was taken to a loving Methodist children's home, also in southern California. There, after public school, I would walk past the La Verne public library where I was at last allowed to freely take out books — exploring stories of the early American pioneers who traveled out west in horse-drawn covered wagons, enduring hardships in following their dreams.

prayers of forgiveness
and the soul of a witness
etched in my coloring book
hidden under the bed
memory of Vista
child's scrapbook of memory

My New Blue Dress

At Vista Del Mar I was tall for my age, and considered chubby. Sometimes we would get hand-me-down clothes from other children in the area, donated by their families and various charities.

Occasionally, one child from Vista would wear a dress or a blouse or trousers and another child in the public school, someone from a family, would recognize their old clothing, things that had been passed on to us. At other times, the clothing came from people who didn't know us kids personally. People who wanted to help, people who were willing to care about us, we were told.

Because I was tall for my age and plump, I was unable to fit into some of the outfits that were donated to us in our age group for Cottage Eleven. Other children had Sunday visits where their parents helped to buy them clothes whenever needed.

So on at least one occasion, my birth mother was allowed to take me shopping. This was not a fun visit for either of us as she had been firmly instructed that her purpose was to find a dress for me and some play clothes. No socializing was permitted. Not even a cup of tea. Time was very limited. This was a weekday outing. Maybe we did get to have a snack together, yet that was breaking the rules.

I think we found some things, in the chubby section of a store. Clothes for a large child were hard to find and more expensive. My mother was not at all comfortable shopping with me, and she had lost all sense of bonding and social intimacy with me on a personal level, even for this sort of basic necessity. At least I felt this way. Of course, she suffered, too.

The day was a day of deep disappointment for both my mother and myself. We were less bonded by then and the lack of success in shopping seemed to reflect something unspoken yet lost forever between us, the mother-daughter connection.

Eventually, during our brief visits, I became less responsive. I withdrew. Where in the world was I? How did I even manage to learn at school. Only God knows.

Later someone brought a beautiful sky blue dress for me to wear. One of the Cottage Eleven housemothers or someone else at Vista, maybe Mrs. T or one of the housemothers for the teenagers, had the insight to bring this to Cottage Eleven for me.

Or maybe my birth father had given money for this new dress. I loved this blue dress and I was eager to wear it to school and then to the afternoon weekday visit with Anne, my mother. Even if the dress had been purchased by someone else, not Anne.

Our visits were infrequent. The court usually allowed her to see me only about ten minutes at a time, and then later, for thirty minutes at a time, at Vista. Often these visits were supervised by a social worker or a probation officer, to make sure I was not told anything that would upset me concerning the tense family situation between my birth parents.

After public school, in my new blue dress, I came back to Cottage Eleven for a snack and to put some school things away. I remember the housemother made sure I would be going to the office. She didn't usually have to remind me of these brief visits so I was somewhat frightened.

She said she had been given a note and someone from the office had also phoned to make sure I showed up. She revealed nothing else, even though she may have been given more information. Often the level of communication between myself and the housemothers became strained.

I desperately needed an adult to bond with, yet there was a lack of trust due to the family circumstances and the changing rules for my supposed sense of well-being. Changes that a child between the ages of seven and ten could not always understand, although people attempted many times to explain things to me.

I walked over to the office where I was scheduled to have the appointment with my mother. The probation officer was there instead. She had something important to tell me. At least she didn't just write an impersonal note and give it to the housemother or the office receptionist!

I braced myself. She offered me a bag of snacks and some pens and pencils and a few picture postcards from my mother and my Aunt Mary. Then Mrs. Greene, very serious and business like, glancing briefly at her watch to note that I was on time, said she could only stay a few minutes, she was running late and had to catch up on a few last appointments.

"I don't have only you as a client," she said. "Well," she smiled, "I see all kinds of people. All sorts." She lit a cigarette. "This is the first real break I have had all day." I offered her some of the fresh fruit my mother had sent.

"I have some hard news for you, Sharon. The court has suspended visits from your mother until this thing is settled. Your father has petitioned that now that your mother is allowed to see you, he wants to visit you as well. Until the court decides, neither parent is allowed to see you."

Again she glanced quickly at her watch. She put out her cigarette. "Thank you for the apple," she said. "I have been so busy today with all these cases I haven't had a chance to eat very much. Your mother says to say she hopes to see you soon. And soon, you most likely will see your father as well. The case will be settled soon. Your psychiatrist, Dr. Miller, is working on this with your parents and the judge. Good luck! That's a pretty blue dress. I wish I had a camera, I would take your picture. Bye."

With time to spare before dinner, I walked over to the teenager's lodge. After school, I would sometimes go there. The teenagers were dancing to 1950's rock and roll music on a record player. They were playing a popular song, "Silhouettes on the Shade."

"What's in the bag, Sharon?" someone asked. I said I had seen my mom and she had given me some postcards. "Want to watch the Loretta Young Show, it's coming on just now," someone said.

With her long dark hair, beautiful eyes and high cheek bones, Loretta Young reminded me of my mother, Anne. So did Queen Elizabeth, a symbolic, nurturing mother figure for me at the time.

Dancing in the teenager's lodge, watching television, I got a needed respite from the dullness of Cottage Eleven, the conformity, the cynicism of the housemother, the depersonalization, the feeling of being anonymous. Sometimes when I was upset, the teenagers were even sympathetic. They forgot about their own problems for awhile, trying to teach me how to dance or to play a game of cards or offering me some chewing gum or a soda.

A Hidden Memory

One weekend afternoon, I came back alone to Cottage Eleven after playing outside. The housemother on duty that day wasn't around. A boy was in the hallway. We were looking for someone to give us our afternoon snacks. I decided to go back to my small dorm room to find something to do. I had already been reading my book and playing outside.

For some reason, I decided this was my time to take a private shower, without the other Cottage Eleven girls around. As I took off my clothes and put on my robe to walk into the girl's bathroom, one of the boys, who wasn't supposed to be in the girl's room, I noticed, had been watching me. Suddenly he called out, "Hey guys, someone's here!"

"There she is. Let's take off her robe!" Two more boys pushed open the bedroom door and tried to open my robe. I screamed. The boys started running away. I closed my robe up and then slowly went back to the shower and turned on the water, thinking I was safe. No one seemed to be around. Yet when they heard the water, the boys came into the bathroom. They had been secretly waiting to see what would happen.

Wearing my robe, I screamed again, then ran into the shower. The two boys fled. Another had stayed in the hall. Later, no one at first believed me or did anything about this. Then, "Maybe you wanted them to give you some attention," a housemother said.

When they didn't believe me, I complained to Mr. Bonapart and to Mr. Maloff, the director and his assistant, telling their secretary what had happened. She said I needed an appointment or a houseparent's note. I went there with two of my girl friends and we also left a note. They had seen my distress and how no one had punished the boys, who teased and harassed them, too. The girls were often blamed for the boys behavior.

Later, my two girl friends, who were sisters, told their father and only then were the boys punished, with no allowance and spankings. Yet I always felt disappointed — no one in authority really seemed to care about the way I was being treated. I still remember how frightened I was when I screamed for help and no one saw what had happened to me.

Since I didn't see my parents as often as most of the other children in Cottage Eleven, I was more vulnerable to abuse. I had liked the little boy who was initially in the hallway with me — I think he told the other two boys they could see me because he was someone who also needed approval and attention. I was around nine years old at the time. I think this was a turning point for my prayed for departure from the home.

collecting inventing revealing
healing concealing exploring
rehabilitation renewal Tikkun Olam

About My Mother

Some of the time, I believed I wouldn't see her again.

looking out from the patio
onto the highway
and I'd imagine
I could see her car

my little child's mind
knew this wasn't true
of course

One day, years later, I did see her, driving past me, on the lookout. To my surprise, she was driving near the pathway to the next door convent. I was walking "home" after school. Her sister and her mother were also in the car. They waved to me. We spoke quickly and quietly. No one must know they had seen me.

Rude Boy at Vista

God bless Arthur
Blessed Be
the man-child at Vista
who intimidated me

he went home to his aunt and uncle
on weekends
while I was all alone
until the glare and the stare

when he and the other kids
on Sunday afternoon
returned to the children's home

until then the glare and the stare
began again

the guitar picking flare
the housemother loved his songs
to her he did no wrong

Yet Arthur had a mean streak. Glad he finally left Cottage Eleven and went to live "up in the home" with the older kids. Even then I knew that he needed help. He was too old and too bad to stay longer in Cottage Eleven. I still wish and wonder if anyone else except me could see that he needed help.

Our time alone interrupted just in time by the nurse at the infirmary on her daily rounds.

someone noticed
someone cared
my story was told
my life was spared

God bless Arthur
Blessed Be
the man-child at Vista
a fateful memory

A Dream for Clarity

This Sunday morning, my life was transformed by an image of Arthur, a rude boy at Vista. He appeared to me just seconds before I woke up, a life-sized adult with long waving hair, Arthur all dressed in white.

The image of Arthur seemed to have a gold luminous light, surrounding his image. The image was there for a mere time, perhaps only one minute. Like a card of the tarot, perhaps representing transformation. Then in a flash he was unseen, and yet, I felt perfect resolution.

Walking Home from School

walking home from school
back to the Jewish children's home
a corner deli
a pickle for a nickel

that salty taste treat
to spice the sour
taste of institutional life

a nickel saved
from lunch time change
saved maybe from
the large oatmeal cookies
someone gifted me

saving
trading
exchanging

The Silent Ring

I

I was ready to seal the envelope
the small package to a friend
poetry — letters — a postcard
of the elegant Indianapolis
train station dining room

something missing —
I opened the envelope
and added one more gift —
children's poems by E.E. Cummings

living in that place
as a child

where visits letters
phone calls were
restricted or non-existent

depending on the
social worker and the judge

I still see the
long — forgotten child

yet now she is home
and happy within me

the letter gets mailed on time

II

up on the hill
away from us
that's where the bad boys lived

juvenile delinquents
some with criminal records

they weren't allowed to
socialize with us kids

they couldn't even go swimming
with us

I used to look up
on that hill
and wonder what their
lives were like

I heard they went to
school where they lived
private teachers for them
up on the hillside

a lone square house
funny glass windows
occasional radio or whistle
like a bullhorn

after awhile I forgot
about that house on the hill
like we weren't supposed
to know or ask about it

yet what was it those
kids could have done
to keep them inside all the time

there were rumors
and one kid lived with us
who was too young
to go up the hill

III

"up in the home"
is where the older teenagers lived

one girl, Maxine,
smoked Camel cigarettes in secret

I saw her and her friends on weekends
when I couldn't see my parents

she made me promise not
to tell on her that she smoked

"Silhouettes On the Shade"
"See You In September"
playing in the lodge

after school I went to the lodge
I liked to watch
"The Loretta Young Show"
and "I Led Three Lives"

Loretta Young on the television
reminded me of my mother

and "I Led Three Lives"
about a secret agent
reminded me of I don't know what

one day I asked one housemother
"What is a communist?"
because on the television show
the actor played one

She said,
"Someone who is different."
yet she hesitated
faltered before answering
as if she didn't really know

I also watched "The Millionaire"
before walking back to
Cottage Eleven to help set
the dinner tables

there was a lone parrot
in the dining room
her name was Chatter

I remember finishing after dinner chores in the Cottage Eleven dining room and then I would cover Chatter's parrot cage with a cloth for the evening.

I also had a little cat
as a friend
Taffy got lost one day

someone said the boys in
Cottage Eleven put her on a train

"Don't take it personally"
one housemother said,
"they are just being boys
someone will find Taffy
and take her to a new home."

my friend Claire at public school
brought her turtle to visit
there were initials carved
on the turtle's shell

Claire invited me
to her house yet I
couldn't go — house
rules and no one to
drive me

so we played with marbles
in the school courtyard,
petted the turtle and Claire
always said hello during our
recess, even when she
was hurrying home
at the end of the day.

Claire and the Turtle

Claire lived near the schoolyard. She brought her ancient turtle for us to see during recess or lunchtime.

The turtle had a name, Evangeline, and she had markings on her shell to tell her age. "We don't know if it's a boy or a girl, we think a girl," Claire said.

Me with my five cents oatmeal cookie I bought in the school cafeteria and a paper bag lunch from the children's home with rotting avocado from our tree and awful cheese.

Claire was kind and I liked her turtle pet. Then she had to carry it home before recess or lunch time ended, sometimes inviting me to visit after school. This was not allowed, children's home rule!

In fourth grade
I often fell asleep
the teacher was indifferent

too much wheat and milk
for my chubby kapha self

walking home I passed
by a railroad track
and a manhole
near a candy factory
where they made Tootsie Rolls

one day the manhole was
open for repair
and we kids looked
into the hole

for some unknown reason
the smell of Tootsie Roll candy
filled the air

bringing a little sweetness
and mystery in our
crowded southern California
desolation

There was a ladder attached to the open manhole and they let us look down yet we could not step on the ladder or go down inside.

Once or twice, or maybe forever, the workmen gave us kids some Tootsie Roll pops. And we sometimes found a few left for us atop the manhole, or around the edges, when they knew we would be passing by on our way home from school.

in school I sat next
to a child actor
Flip Mark
when they were filming
"Please Don't Eat the Daisies"
with Doris Day and David Niven

once also, a Hollywood studio
filmed scenes at the children's home, for
a movie,"The Gift of Love"
with Lauren Bacall, Robert Stack and Evelyn Rudie

so that in the strange
and strained landscape
of our childhood
we had a little life of fantasy

when I watch
this movie on television
I see the landscape
the children's home
where we lived

I wish that I could
recognize the faces
of the kids I knew from Vista
who were chosen to act in the film

maybe there was a reason
they edited those brief scenes

maybe like for so many
years I tried to edit
my childhood from memory
a strange and hidden reality

how I longed to be
one of the children
on the Art Linkletter show

the Hollywood talent scouts came
to our school
looking for children

the shy girl was pretty
yet not interested
the small boy
awkward yet chosen
and how cute

I was of course
too plump too chubby
too curly too tall
for the producers of the show

I still liked that show
yet thought I could do better
than the kids they chose
as best for starship encounters
in the playground of L.A.
where coincidence can still
make you "Queen for a Day."

An Undiscovered Melody

Looking back on this time of utter aloneness and childhood desolation, I think one of the most painful aspects of this experience was the complete absence of any adult or parent figure with whom I could share my daily activities, achievements and little successes — such as a good mark in school, a new friend, the discovery of special blossoms, flowers on a tree.

From the vantage point of now, I am still overcome with the bleakness of those years. A photo of me at Vista Del Mar shows me as happy. Yet the photo is not real. I was posed to smile and to have my hands on the piano keys. I don't play piano. The early family music experiences were not continued once I was taken to Vista.

As far as I know or can remember, there was no process or opening for me, or for anyone else, to enjoy music lessons. The lone exception was Arthur, an older boy in Cottage Eleven who played guitar and sang.

Later, with my adoptive family, and also, living on my own, I attempted to study music, with mixed results. I had emotional difficulty with piano lessons. Although I wanted to learn, there was something that kept me away. For awhile I played guitar.

Yet music continues to be a healing influence for me, even without formal accomplishment. Listening, playing percussion, studying, performing and teaching creative dance, my jazz-poetry and liturgical prayer celebrations, the song poems in my experimental plays and children's writings — these pleasures are always in my life.

Before I was sent to Vista Del Mar I recall the nature walks with my Aunt Mary in the Pacific Palisades Park in Santa Monica, California. And I also recall the tenderness that she showed me when she taught me notes on the white and black piano keys, and her early realization that I could play music by ear. My mother Anne also played piano by ear and her love of music and singing lullabies to me inspired me. Both my birth parents enjoyed classical music as well. Perhaps some of the beginnings of my later song poems and the stories and poems I have written for young children have their start in these early events.

Thank you, Meher Baba, for my connection to artistic expression. Amid the turmoil, I am grateful that this source of creativity in my life has helped to sustain me.

As a Child

Even with the tumultuous memories and feelings, I can still recall some happiness with my birth family.

at first I did not know
the names of trees
I loved the wind
the garden breeze

watched and waved
to the trains passing by
while I watered
peach and plum tree

the small child pond
the West Los Angeles sun
our home
on Ashby Lane

An Orphan and Her Cat

Taffy the calico cat lived near Vista Del Mar Children's Home. She would visit us, especially during the day. I would come "home" from public school to find her at the front door of Cottage Eleven, waiting to greet me. I would take her round the place to the kitchen, where Mrs. Cook set out a special dish of milk and kitchen scraps and sometimes gave me a cookie, too.

In the weed patch in back, outside the kitchen, Mrs. Cook planted wild catnip for Taffy. She explained to me that cats may enjoy this plant and some will eat the leaves. Taffy spent more time with me than with the other kids. Perhaps she sensed I didn't have visits from my parents on weekends, like the other children. The housemother, Mrs. Katz, encouraged me to play with Taffy, even though pets weren't usually invited to the cottage.

One day, Taffy cat came round wearing a little bell on a red ribbon around her neck. Next I knew, Taffy went away. Her people moved out of town. We pretended Taffy ran away, boarding the local train at the station down the road from the children's home. A group of boys said they saw Taffy riding away in a boxcar.

We pretended to ride away on a train with Taffy. I missed her and yet, somehow, I was glad she was gone. Yet she was my only companion. There was no one else. Maybe I really wished her presence to be secret. A secret companion who kept me company during my long childhood days with no parents.

invisible special silent
now that you're gone
someone else finds me

a hidden place
no one can see
only you and me

Milt Davis Stories

Hold Your Tongue

So what was I to do with this little voice inside me, arriving at odd hours and seeming to say to me, "Tell my story." I finally decided not to ignore her.

Toward the end of my stay at Vista, when I was nine years old, the housemother announced one night that, "We will be having a gourmet specialty surprise tonight for our dinner. Mrs. Cook will bring to the table a special tomato and meat stew. I think you will enjoy this meal very much."

Mrs. Katz spoke in her heavy Czechoslovakian accent. We were hoping against hope for something good to eat. Mrs. Cook, with an apologetic smile on her face, attempting to look happy and hopeful, brought the large steaming cauldron into the dining room and set the concoction in front of Mrs. Katz. There was a large ladle, we each had a glass of milk and plenty of fresh bread and butter.

"Oh no," Susie made an unpleasant looking grimace. "I bet that we are having tongue again."

Susie had a strong sense of smell and could tell beforehand, somehow, what we were having for dinner, and whether or not we would have something delicious like spaghetti or something so awful we would pretend to chew it and then hide it in our napkins.

Milt Davis, our part-time housefather, strode into the dining hall. "All right you kids," he said. "No monkey business. Time to eat if you want dessert and outdoor time." He was very serious and yet we felt a connection to him. We were told he was a star football player, and that he worked at the children's home during the off-season.

We kids soon discovered the awful truth about our food that night. The tongue was in disguise. Hidden in a vat of tomato sauce. We quickly and secretly collected all the napkins that we could. Now everyone knew exactly what to do. Except for shy and quiet little Maurice, who seemed to enjoy the meal.

For the rest of us, there was bread and butter and milk and string beans for dinner. And if we were lucky, an apple that wasn't rotten. Each of us hid the supposedly eaten tongue in our napkins, and slipped it under the table into our pockets, to take outside quickly and quietly after the evening meal, to hide in the bushes during our outdoor after dinner playtime. Even Milt Davis looked the other way.

We called it the "mystery meal." After awhile, after what seemed like a really long time, the food at the home got better. Enough kids complained to their parents about the Vista meals, (especially lunch and dinner) over their weekly telephone conversations and during overnight weekends and Sunday visits.

My birth father complained that we had such awful food because the director — our overseer — went to Hawaii on a fancy vacation so we didn't get better food or a chance to go to summer camp. Vista made changes when parents complained loud and a lot.

Small changes like good food, caring compassionate house — mothers, better care for me and the other kids who didn't get to go home for Sundays and overnight visits with parents — changes of the heart would have made a big difference in our lives, in all our lives, even up 'til now.

pick up sticks
lunch time gifts

tether ball and jacks
off beat snacks

at the children's home
my love for God
tested to the max

childhood games
within the frame
of His Remembrance

A Vista Birthday

At Vista Del Mar Children's Home, unlike most of the other children in Cottage Eleven, I was not permitted to celebrate my birthday with my family. A brief phone call or a card with a gift were the only ways my parents could wish me a happy birthday during those years at Vista. After visits with my father resumed, he was once again permitted to give me birthday gifts and presents for other holidays.

One year on my birthday, when I was eight or nine years old, I was feeling somewhat frantic, depressed and alone. I thought to myself, what an awful time! We'll probably have a terrible dinner and maybe someone will light a candle. Will anyone even remember or bring a cake for me? There was no one to share my despair with, because my next therapy session wasn't until the next week. Or, perhaps there was a counseling session that week, yet what could the psychiatrist do to make up for this loss, the emptiness I was living, experiencing?

None of the housemothers had the professional insight, empathy and love that many of us children so desperately required in our lives to simply function. I often shared yet received unsatisfactory responses or none at all. Once, after I had been at the home for only a few weeks, the resident housemother, Anna Katz, tired of my tears, told me I was too sensitive.

In the following years, I bonded with Anna in a way. Once, on a weekend when the other children were away visiting their families, I was even permitted to watch television and look through the magazines and newspapers in her private suite. My father had gifted Anna with flowers and chocolates for Valentine's Day; his way of silently pleading for some degree of attention for his daughter.

My birth father, Leonard, an Orthodox Jew and a capmaker in his family business, became friendly with another father. Mr. Sushan had two daughters at Vista. One of the girls, Harriet, had what we called spells. She actually had epilepsy.

I was friendly with Harriet and her older sister, Judy. On Sundays, Mr. Sushan would come to greet the girls and they would go out with him for the day. My father contacted Mr. Sushan and they began comparing notes about the difficult conditions in the home, the lack of good food, clothes, the absence of love, special attention and nurturing.

The friendship between my father and Mr. Sushan caused something of a stir. I believe that this was the beginning of my father's full-fledged motivation to have me removed from Vista. His complaints to various public authorities eventually were successful.

Another child that I liked was named Ronnie. He was very intelligent, and unlike most of the other children, Ronnie also loved to read and sometimes had to read in secret. He arrived at the home after I had somewhat adjusted and been there awhile. Ronnie soon began to obsessively touch, lick and bite his arm, even though the housemothers and his social worker were alerted to make him avoid this behavior.

I liked Ronnie because he seemed creative, sensitive and different from the other children. Ronnie became friends with a child named Allen Salter, and soon they and their parents were visiting together on Sundays and holiday weekends. Like my father and Mr. Sushan, Ronnie and Allen's parents also heard stories about what was unfair and lacking in the home. The combination of more than one parent hearing all these complaints gave more validation and importance to the issues.

It wasn't just one kid complaining or exaggerating.

As a way to help the situation, my birth father was encouraged to continue to help by giving holiday gifts to me and others. For my birthday, there was a big surprise when we entered the dining room that evening. I still remember how we each had different rotating household chores and each evening, one of us would call out, while ringing the bells, "Dinner, dinner, last call for dinner."

This evening, my birthday, there were individual bottles of Coca-Cola waiting for each child, beside our dinner plates and our bread plates. The part-time housefather, Milt Davis walked into the dining room and beamed when he saw the Coca-Cola bottles. "What's all this for? We just had Christmas, I mean Chanukah," he joked.

Mrs. Katz motioned toward me. "Oh, it's for you. Ok, here we go," he said. He found the bottle opener and walked around to each of us, around twelve children, preparing to carefully open the cokes.

"Now you kids," he said strictly, "You can only have these cokes if you promise to eat your dinner. In fact, I am going to wait until you all eat most of your dinner before I open these drinks."

"Is this girl getting gifts this year? Lord, I hope so," he said as he silently crossed himself.

"Thank you, God, for this blessing," he said quietly.

Yes, thank you God. Someone, somewhere, somehow had provided a beautiful birthday cake with vanilla icing, pink roses and birthday candles. Mrs. Cook, one of my favorite people, was beaming as she brought out the cake, with the birthday candles lit by Mrs. Katz.

After I blew out the candles, Mrs. Katz smiled at me and said, "Now Sharon, who do you think gave these birthday treats to you? It was your father. He wanted us to surprise you. Aren't you happy?" And she handed me the birthday card signed by him.

I was happy and I was distraught. For years, my birth mother, grandmother and aunt had darkly warned me that if I ever ate any of the treats my father gave to me (such as peanuts and popcorn on his visits) I would probably die. They said he wanted to kill me.

A voice inside me said what they had brainwashed me to believe, "Don't eat — it's poison." Frightened and scared, I ran from the table, carefully hiding the slice of chocolate birthday cake with vanilla icing and a pink rose inside my napkin, preparing to throw it away as I and the other kids did when we got something we couldn't stand to eat.

At the same time, I knew that the other children were enjoying my favorite ice cream that my father had lovingly remembered for me, Neapolitan.

There was a knock on the door of the girl's dormitory room where I had sequestered myself. I closed my eyes, wishing I could disappear, yet at the same time grateful for the attention, as one of the children, a friend, spoke quietly, saying, “Read this.” The note she gave me said, “Hurry up and join us.” The houseparents and my Vista Del Mar birthday substitute ‘family’ were asking me to come back to the table.

Grateful for the response, yet reluctant, I walked with my friend into the dining room to join the other children.

“Now Sharon, we are so very happy that you came back here before all the other kids had time to finish eating your birthday dessert and hiding or opening your presents,” Milt Davis said with a serious concern.

What is your problem, miss?” asked someone, one of the kids. “Don’t you like your dad’s gifts for your birthday? We sure do.” I didn’t want to tell my terrible secret, which just then, I hardly believed myself. For if all these other kids were eating these delicious treats, then they would die as well.

Thank God for the strict yet loving encouragement from Milt Davis, and for the enjoyment of the other kids who were happily and quietly eating in the total silence of his dinner rule for this bizarre occasion. I finally was feeling safe enough to sit down, relax and enjoy the dessert. And besides, how could Coca-Cola be poison when one had to use a bottle opener to get it opened?

When I finally opened the birthday gifts my father had sent me, everyone applauded. One of the gifts was a small and brand new flashlight, for a special secret project I had been planning.

Milt Davis thanked the Lord again, and then he kissed the crucifix he wore around his neck. I somehow understood this serious and important action since I had sometimes observed and spoken with the nuns who lived in the convent next door to the children’s home. Cathy, my best friend at Vista, was Catholic and she had whispered to me often about Jesus Christ her savior and of her longing to once again celebrate Christmas.

I believe that Milt Davis brought to me and this entire situation a blessing and that his heartfelt prayers to Jesus helped me survive life at Vista Del Mar.

"Okay, kids," Milt Davis said "Listen up. Say thank you to Sharon and her dad. Maybe someday you all will understand what happened here tonight."

+ Milton Eugene Davis, PhD (May 31, 1929–September 29, 2008) was an All-Pro defensive back for the Baltimore Colts who played on two National Football League championship teams and twice led the league in interceptions. He worked at the Vista Del Mar Jewish Children's Home as a houseparent and counselor while in college and also in off-season from football. He had lived at Vista as a child himself. He left professional football to get a doctorate in education at UCLA and later became a college professor.

"thank you God"

thank you God
thanks be to God
for the crystals
for the prayer beads
for the healing touch
of the Rosary

the wintergreen
the rain on the Sarcococca tree
and your everlasting love

VII. Hours of Prayer

The prayer that God hears is the prayer of the heart, that suffering of the heart is what God pays attention to.

— Meher Baba,
Meher Baba Calling, p. 36

Prayer and Trust, Talking To God

Whatever happened at Vista, certain places, meadows, trees, corners, clouds and people were definitely safer than others. Certain noises, smells, sounds were definitely not to be trusted.

I trusted the books on the bookshelf, especially Nancy Drew and *The Sea for Sam*. I trusted a few children friends and I trusted Mrs. Cook. Sometimes it's the people in the background who are not directly involved in any special agenda or expectation who help the most — the housemother I could visit "up in the home" who stayed with the older kids, Mrs. Cook, who was our Cottage Eleven cook, Mrs. T in her office of candy and other supplies, Cindy and Axel in the laundry, Al who volunteered on Saturdays and took us to Knott's Berry Farm, on picnics and to Disneyland.

In my walk back to the children's home from public school, I began searching the sidewalk pavement for some sort of significance in found change, in the littered streets, old chewing gum, candy wrappers, a smile. One day I found that I could walk through the grounds of the Nazareth Convent, a place of peace, contentment and mystery. I saw comfort and acceptance there. The nuns were a strong symbol of love.

Praying to God and trusting in Him is what I believe sustained me at Vista Del Mar Children's Home, when my family visits were so erratic, chaotic and unpredictable. I was influenced by the girl next to me in our small dormitory, who I recently discovered is Catholic. This was unusual. I believe that God placed me next to this child, (we both arrived at the home on the same week), to learn about Jesus and to have compassion for the other, for Catherine James was an outsider, being the only non-Jewish child.

Walking sometimes through the convent grounds on my short walk from public school back to the Jewish children's home, I may have glimpsed the nuns and spoke with them occasionally, in the nearby Nazareth convent. The sense of safety, beauty and mystery I experienced there gives me a feeling of gratitude and of admiration for the Catholic faith.

Hully Gully

Once we girls danced to a rock and roll song, *The Hully Gully*. The housemother saw us and told us to stop immediately. Except for this one time, the housemother was always kind and enthusiastic. This was during my six-month stay at the second place, the Methodist David and Margaret Children's Home in La Verne, California. Aside from this one time, I really loved the place. I didn't have any idea why we needed to avoid dancing, since we were enjoying ourselves. A few of the other girls who had been living there a longer time seemed to understand, however.

"Girls, I'm surprised at the way you are carrying on, dancing like this. This is not the Christian way to behave." Our housemother started to walk away, and then, "Sharon, I am especially surprised at you. This is not the behavior I expect from you and the other girls. You should know better, and let me know if this happens again. I want you girls to let me know if you find someone continuing to dance like this, and to avoid this kind of dancing. This is not what we do here at the David and Margaret Home, and most of you have been here long enough to know that this is a sin. Girls, your behavior is sinful."

She may have actually warned us about going to heaven, and isn't that what we wished for, and therefore we needed to be good. She was surprised at my dancing with the other girls because I was usually quiet and shy. Dance is a form of celebration and prayer and we girls were bonding as well.

"thank you Holy One"

thank you Holy One
for all you have
done for me
and for all
that you haven't done
in your name and Love
Amen

explore the Rosary
praying with the Rosary beads
praying with prayer beads
beginning to innovate
new and ancient ways

to see and to honour
His holy way
build a walking Rosary garden
a walking way to pray
blessings in His name
Amen

In Jesus Name

One Sunday, while I stood, waiting and admiring the pastoral Christ painting in the hallway to the dining area at David and Margaret Children's Home, a Sunday visitor stood next to me and smiled, "Sometimes things happen to us that we don't understand," he said kindly. "Yet years later, we find the purpose."

I was astonished since I hardly ever heard anyone tell me about God or speak in such profound philosophical terms. For years I had prayed to God to release me from the suffering, isolation and blunders of institutional life at Vista. I had prayed to be able to see my family. Now I was in a new children's home with a new "family." They were all Christian.

I felt so grateful, relieved God had answered my prayers. The food was better, the clothes were prettier, the kids seemed less troubled, the housemothers less like dictators. There were more and longer family visits. At last, I was a happy child, again, to some extent, in some ways.

Several months ago, I noticed that the Christian hymn, "Praise God From Whom All Blessings Flow" is now included in the early Sunday morning service at St. Paul's Episcopal Church, where we sing this song after communion. To my surprise, I knew this hymn by heart. Tears came to my eyes as I was easily able to sing along, recalling the words and the melody. I believe that we would sing this hymn every Sunday as Grace before our noon meal at the second place I lived as a child, the David and Margaret Home, which was a Methodist residence for children.

+ Praise God, from whom all blessing flow
Praise Him, all creatures here below
Praise Him above, ye heavenly host
Praise Father, Son and Holy Ghost. Amen
— Words by Anglican Bishop Thomas Ken

Sanctuary

I feel that I found God at Vista Del Mar and then at the David and Margaret Methodist Children's Home. Every loss I experienced, every loneliness, every grief, grievance, whim, wish and fancy, I began to give to the Lord. More and more, gifts of love, peace and understanding enter my heart when I begin, again and again, to know and to see that every action is Him — to see my entire life this way.

The longing for my mother and the aloneness led me to pray to God — the sense of total abandonment led me, as a young child, to ask, to plead, "Dear God, please help me to be able to go home. Please help me to leave this place."

Yet the God I prayed to was not of a specific religion, the God was the God of hope. And eventually my prayers were answered, yet not as I had consciously anticipated.

Those long years, age seven to ten without family, I prayed for God to help me to be able to leave the children's institution and to see my family. My inner prayers were deeply significant. They helped me to survive the trauma of family separation. The prayers were a conversation between me and God. The prayers were different than the formal ones we learned in Sunday school, the ones we said on the Jewish sabbath and Jewish holidays at Vista Del Mar.

My childhood prayers were a private chapel of love between me and God, to help me. They were and are His gift, His blessing, His unfathomable grace. I may never be able to completely understand the significance of the events or the karma that I lived through as a child.

At times, when I felt God wasn't answering my personal entreaties, I felt a deep rift, a sense of loss. Sometimes this bereavement still permeates my life; appearing, then disappearing and then making a new entrance. In this life I search for and I find, with Meher Baba's help, various ways to throw off the mask of illusion, various ways to reclaim the holy encounter with God, breath by breath.

My prayers at that time in my life are an early source for my current writings, especially my devotional prayer poems. Through my stories, collage art, dance and holistic health research, I find strength and compassion toward myself and to inspire others. At the age of seven, in the midst of my loneliness and isolation, God gave me the gift of prayer, the gift of trust, the gift of His remembrance. I see this gift in my life today.

Meher Baba's hand in these stories now seems like a hidden love letter quietly emerging as I revisit memories and experiences, sometimes with additional fancy. From those early years, a place for prayer is the gift from Him that I have been able to hold on to.

Thank You, Lord Meher Baba.

Mary's Song, the Magnificat (A Catholic Hymn)

My soul doth glory in Your love, O Lord.
My soul doth glory in Your love, O Lord.
For You gazed on your servant with compassion, and
You reached out and took me by the hand.
Great are you, God, and Holy is Your name.
Your mercy reaches to the end of time.
Ah, the lowly You raise to the heavens, and the
proud-hearted have no part with You.
Ah, how you fill the hungry with Your love.
With empty hands the rich are sent away.
You will always be mindful of Your mercy, as You
promised Your people long ago.
My soul doth glory in Your love, O Lord.
My soul doth glory in Your love, O Lord.
For You smiled on Your servant with compassion, and
You reached out and took me by the hand.

+ During the Saturday evening Vigil Mass at my neighborhood Catholic Church, I heard this song, we sang it as a hymn. The words touched me. I had only several days previously written that I believe Meher Baba reached out his hand to deliver me from the suffering I experienced at Vista Del Mar.

A Weekend Serenade

from the local consignment shop
this lovely little cloth bag I just found

the clasp and the knob
appear difficult at times
to close

like your heart
the Lord tells me

this other bag
that you almost bought
has a clasp
that is easier to close

yet you were right
to wait around the shop
looking like a waif
until I gave you the clue
for this bag that is just for you

this bag with the lovely
embroidered flower design
you just bought
also has a slightly discolored place
you didn't notice at first
and so does your heart

the stain that I have cleansed
for you

although the small consignment shop
has no name
the owner is not to blame

Lord Meher Baba
I took your name
all around town
now I am tired
and almost lame
from all the walking

saying your name
without a rosary
talking to myself
and some people see

the indifference
the Divine Game

the house that was sold
the barking dog
the new owner who smiled
and introduced his pet

the Lord smiles kindly
we are not finished yet.

+ I usually note Labor Day as the time I was driven by the social worker from my birth mother's place to the Vista Del Mar Jewish Children's Home. This poem was written during a Labor Day Weekend, September 5, 2015.

Mirage

these clouds want me to be happy
especially in spring
when you call unexpectedly
at my doorstep
or at the rain-splattered window

or in the solo violin of remembrance
at my brother's music class
and in the tambourine
as I wander these remote desert roads
clouds call to me

a rainbow direction
a confident smile
a mark of your Love
or sometimes hearing your call
even when I don't listen

even in disruption or confusion
even in the still of the night
a new dress rehearsal
or a mysterious view in the stars
a sense of stillness in the sand bar

+ The poet's brother is Joel Daniel Robinson (January 18, 1956–October 31, 1981). May his memory be a blessing.

The Unconventional Prayer

The voice of intuition is my voice.

— Meher Baba

But that angels are for real,
This I've never held in doubt;
Radiant creatures, pure, ideal,
Here on earth they walk about.

— From *The Angels*
by Heinrich Heine

The idea to write this story came to me almost like a dream. Yet this is true.

At age seven when I first arrived at the Jewish children's home, I was assigned to meet with a loving and compassionate red-haired social worker. I do not remember her name. I remember how thoughtful she was. I was so thankful to have a confidant at "the home," a nurturing, kind and caring person. I trusted her. She seemed to understand me and to value me. This was completely unlike the housemothers, who were unable to give me the emotional support that I needed.

Yet the red-haired social worker, even in her professional role, was able to view me, to hear me, to understand me. After a series of sessions with her, as the complexity of my family situation became clear, I was told that I would be instead seeing a psychiatrist. Thereafter, I was bereft of the close companionship, playfulness and light-hearted humor that had graced my visits with the Vista Del Mar social worker.

The absence of an adult companion during my years at Vista was undoubtedly Meher Baba's will. In this suffering and my writing about those times, other gifts surface: my own reservoir of inner healing and concern for others; a window into my past.

I am still affected by those childhood experiences when I was taken to the Los Angeles children's home and the promise to see birth family in a timely fashion was not kept, due to various factors. And although I have forgiven all involved, yet my experience is that a lifetime of inner work is necessary to cope with such a traumatic encounter, one that encompassed several years of my early life. Those years when promised family visits were sporadic and uncertain is even now a basic aspect of my identity.

Years later, in Port Townsend, Washington, I began to speak with Janet Self, RN. She had transitioned from being an allopathic nurse and is now a Holistic nurse and intuitive counselor. We initially met in a local Buddhist sangha, a community for Zen Buddhist meditation in Port Townsend. I was deeply impressed to read her story about working with integrative medicine for her own health challenge, multiple sclerosis.

In writing her story, she was opening a pathway for me. A way that says yes to happiness, joy and wellness, at the same time that I can learn to embrace the commitment that is needed for self-care and professional guidance as my way of life. A poet friend commented about Janet's courage in openly writing about her experiences. Janet was helping my friend Robert Komishane and his mental and physical health was improving. I see now that in writing about herself in this way in a local journal, Janet was also revealing her unique role as an intuitive healer. Her courage and her story open the door to the understanding of my life purpose.

From time to time I asked her about nutrition and supplements, and I began to have counseling sessions with her as well. She was able to give me insights into my own psychic nature and how to handle sensitive aspects of my life so that I can thrive. At the same time, I continued to see my mainstream social worker to help me with my emotional health, the lifelong chronic aftermath of childhood trauma and the effects on my life now. Yet connecting with Janet gives me a different perspective, unique insights, holistic and spiritual support.

In her holistic therapy background, she and I currently have telephone conversations, where I briefly explain a problem to her and then something magical begins. In our prayer time and silence during a consultation, we receive insights and ways to assist me. Gnosis. Baba is at the helm of our work.

As I mentioned, my cherished childhood social worker had red hair and so does Janet. I appreciate Janet's knowledge and I am grateful that while she is helping me and counseling me, she also allows me to discuss my ideas about how to develop our dialogue.

In that way, I am able to use my own discernment, a combination of my inner guidance with Janet's counsel. In this ongoing conversation, by myself, in a counseling session and in life, I am connecting my devotion for Meher Baba and His teachings with the various healing modalities that arrive in my life. In His Love.

The child-like hope that someday a special kind of listener would again enter my life is now returned to me in the answers, in the mystery and in self-realization. Janet, thank you for believing in me. In the aura of the universe, the web of knowledge and inspiration connect us. The missing heart imprint is now being replenished. Meher Baba's love is guiding you.

A Portal to the Unknown

As a child at Vista Del Mar Jewish Children's Home, I thought that my family were no longer living, when I couldn't see them. At the same time, I became more aware of the energies of those around me, including those not physically present. This sensitivity has become more apparent in my adult years. Thanks to more open, inclusive parameters that value intuition, including the teachings of Carl Jung, I am now able to understand my perception as a unique spiritual and psychological strength. I now see myself as a victor.

seen and unseen
visible and invisible
known and yet unknown

AFTERWORD

In the Heart of God

the children's home
is at rest
in a blanket of memory

streaming live
in the California sunshine
in the warmth and challenge
of friendship love and life

wishing to live
to be to endure to share
thank you for visiting me here

Amen

certain things I never learned to do
let that increase my love for you

Goodbye, Vista Del Mar. Things happened so fast that maybe I never really had a chance or the time to say goodbye to you. Yes, I was glad to leave. After living at the David and Margaret Methodist Children's Home, I finally had a new home to go to, with the Robinson family, when we moved to Croton-on-Hudson, New York. Yet I never really processed the mixed sense of sadness and relief I felt in knowing I could leave Vista.

Goodbye, Vista. Thank you, God's Grace, for whatever karma or destiny was worked out in the children's homes. Thank you God, for this experience, for a place to live, with food, clothing, shelter.

Thank you, God. Thank you for these stories, thank you for telling them and letting me share them with the world. Thank you, Vista!

Finding the Lost Tribe of Vista

threads of memory
woven into each page
of these mementoes

someone somewhere who
throughout my life
I always sensed
they were searching

for me lost then found
in my life in my imagination
lost and found
in His Love and Grace

Amen

Even when God is silent, we can always trust that He is with us. During the long years of my stay at Vista Del Mar Children's Home, when family visits were not given to me as they were to the other children in Cottage Eleven, I believe now that I learned to hold fast to Meher Baba's damaan (the hem of His garment, a reference to remembrance of Him). Significant themes in my life and reflections include the aspect of becoming spiritually stronger as a result of this suffering.

As a child I felt and believed that with my continuous and answered prayers, I would be able to leave Vista Del Mar Children's Home. After two and a half years, I was given the chance to live in a better children's home and then to be adopted into the Robinson family.

However, God had a plan for me to live with this new family. He gave me gifts that were not in my prayers. The sense of faith was ongoing in my life as a child resident at Vista, giving me a sense of spiritual strength that lasts for me. Today, I am able to appreciate this experience, emerging from the depths of despair as child waif.

claiming my past
finding voice
Love Alone Prevails

Amen

Thank you, Beloved Meher Baba

Writing this collection brings great awareness and reminds me that my experience in the orphanage brought me closer to God and to prayer. By creating this collection of memories and imagination, I am now able to recall this inner light in my childhood experience. Strands of memory, clues, insights, interpretations and heart felt guidance from the Beloved inform this collection.

My forgiveness. The very situation that is most distressing can be turned around to be a blessing.

In a beautiful yet painful way, God gave those weekend times of utter aloneness and silence at Vista Del Mar.

Yet now and always, the embracing of the love, the pathos and the flowers of those who arranged this journey.

Today perhaps I am free to embrace all the aspects and nuances of this experience.

I am thankful for my adopted parents, Ruth and Rabbi Michael Aaron Robinson, for their courage in taking me into their home.

And for the opportunity to grow up in Croton-on-Hudson, New York, with a special significance for me as a connection to Meher Baba. For Meher Baba stayed there (at that time called Harmon-on-Hudson) during His first visit to the U.S. in 1931 and again in 1932.

As a young woman, I frequently traveled on the Croton-Harmon train into New York City, before I consciously knew about Meher Baba. In His travels, Meher Baba and His disciples rode this train route when He visited our village, years earlier, before I was born. I also walked by the Sing Sing Prison concrete circular wall in Ossining, New York, near the train station, to go home to Croton after work. Baba had been there, too, and described a prisoner within those gates as His agent, an abdal.

to wander
then find yourself
yourself
in the heart of God

Commentary by Judy Alexander, Vista Del Mar Alumna

Many of Sharon's experiences at Vista Del Mar were painful. She could not find compassion there, but did what she could as a young child to make sense of her experiences, and to find solace where she could.

I too am an alumna of Vista Del Mar, living in Cottage eleven from age six to eleven. I moved to another house before Sharon arrived, so we did not know each other, but we do share several memories. While our early childhood trauma had some similarities, how we coped with our abandonment and detachment differed greatly. I was completely withdrawn, stopped talking and almost shut down completely in order to feel safe inside. I share this little bit about myself only to say how taken I am with Sharon's quest to find peace at a young age, and search deep inside for spiritual meaning to all that was happening to her at Vista.

I was fascinated by Sharon's stories about the nuns at the convent behind Cottage thirty-six. Such vivid descriptions of how she was able to find comfort in her imagination of a way of life that held some spiritual truth. I lived in Cottage thirty-six after Cottage eleven, so I was able to watch the nuns a lot. I remember their laughter while playing volleyball. In my own imagination as a child I thought that their whole existence was to be silent and walk around slowly in prayer, so it was a joy to see them playing something that we played in elementary school! But Sharon saw so much more, and followed her heart.

Sharon's stories about her life at Vista Del Mar are sad, but as she pairs them with her poetry, she conveys a deeper meaning of her journey, creativity and spiritual path.

— Anacortes, Washington
June 19, 2021

BIOGRAPHY

Sharon Lia Robinson follows the path of her heart to create innovative cultural connections.

Her dance, films, poems, stories and visual art reflect the search for a sense of belonging and the mystical trip to love, self-acceptance and redemption.

Sharon was a catalyst for the pioneering feminist anthology *Shadow on a Tightrope: Writings by Women on Fat Oppression* (Aunt Lute Books, 1982). Her poetry and essays appear in that collection under her early pen name, Sharon Bas Hannah.

She has directed and produced two documentary films.

In her 2002 film memoir, *My Journey Toward Wholeness* she reflects on life as an artist and her research as an independent scholar for healing of early psychological challenges.

In the 2009 film *Edge of the Sea Gallery* (1998–2003) Sharon documents the art center she developed with visual artist/photographer Steven R. Johnson, as a sanctuary to nurture artists and poets in Port Townsend, Washington.

She has shared her poems in liturgical prayer celebrations, secular places and journals. Her 2017 collection, *Wayward Star, Devotional Poems* is available from Sheriar Books, (843-272-1339) www.sheriarbooks.org

Sharon is inspired by the spiritual teachings of Meher Baba and by Pope Francis, the saints, the poets and the mystical Oneness within all of the major world religions.

Sharon's writings are archived in the Schlesinger Library of the Radcliffe Institute, Harvard University, Cambridge, Massachusetts.

www.sharonrobinson.org

January 19, 1963, Sharon at the Robinson family home, Croton-on-Hudson, New York.

Circa 1963, Sharon with family cat, Tiger, at home in Croton-on-Hudson, New York.

June, 1965, Family at home after Sharon's Confirmation, Croton-on-Hudson, New York. Left to right, Back row, Leah Karpen, (sister of Rabbi Michael A. Robinson), Morris Karpen, (husband of Leah), dad, Rabbi Michael A. Robinson, Grandmother Esther Robinson. Left to right, Front row, brother Joel Daniel Robinson with mom Ruth Robinson, Minnie Tarlov (dad's cousin), Sharon, Manny Tarlov, sister Jude Robinson, unidentified.

This book is set in Minion Pro typeface designed by Robert Slimbach
in 1990 and inspired by late Renaissance-era type.
Titles are set in Barbedor designed by Hans Eduard Meier in 1992.

*

Designed by Cindy Ziegler and printed by
Sheriar Press, 3005 Hwy. 17 North Bypass, Myrtle Beach, SC 29577

With great appreciation and thanksgiving.